BREWING
ECLECTIC
IPA

Pushing the Boundaries of India Pale Ale

BY DICK CANTWELL

BREWERS
PUBLICATIONS™

Brewers Publications™
A Division of the Brewers Association
PO Box 1679, Boulder, Colorado 80306-1679
BrewersAssociation.org
BrewersPublications.com

Proudly printed in the United States of America

10 9 8 7 6 5 4 3 2 1
ISBN-13: 978-1-938469-46-6
Library of Congress Cataloging-in-Publication Data
Names: Cantwell, Dick, author.
Title: Brewing eclectic IPA : pushing the boundaries of India pale ale / by
  Dick Cantwell.
Description: Boulder, Colorado : Brewers Publications, a division of the
  Brewers Association, [2018] I Includes bibliographical references and
  index.
Identifiers: LCCN 2017060186 I ISBN 9781938469466 (pbk. : alk. paper)
Subjects: LCSH: Ale. I Microbreweries.
Classification: LCC TP578 .C36 2018 I DDC 663/.42--dc23 LC record available at
  https://lccn.loc.gov/2017060186

Publisher: Kristi Switzer
Technical Editors: Mitch Steele, Lindsay Barr
Copyediting: Iain Cox
Indexing: Doug Easton
Art Direction: Jason Smith
Graphic Design: Danny Harms
Production: Justin Petersen
Cover Photo: Luke Trautwein

To my sources.

TABLE OF CONTENTS

FOREWORD

In the 40 years or so that American craft brewing has been in existence, one thing that has remained constant is the incredible rate at which change occurs in this industry and how quickly preferences for certain beer flavors and beer styles can change. In the beginning, in the late 1970s and early to mid-1980s, most craft brewers were brewing in the English style, brewing Americanized versions of British ales, such as pale ales, ESBs, porters, and stouts. Many brewpubs in those days offered up just three beers: a golden ale, an amber ale, and a dark ale. But being curious and passionate about beer and brewing history, homebrewers and professional brewers continued to research traditional beer styles. They discovered the story of India pale ale (IPA) and then attempted to brew their own versions. Some early craft brewers were old enough to remember the last traditionally brewed IPA in the United States, Ballantine IPA, which provided an inspiration as well. It was simply a natural progression that the new IPA style, brewed with an abundance of American hops, eventually made its way into the lineup of several breweries.

Craft brewers continue pushing the envelope of flavor, adopting new and unusual ingredients that expand the boundaries of classic beer styles while at the same time demonstrating reverence for the beers that have come before them. This willingness to take risks has driven the growth of craft beer, as people have gradually rediscovered flavor and rejected blandness in their food and drink choices over the past few decades. As the craft beer industry has grown and matured, it has been very interesting to watch what beers styles and fads have come and gone. Who remembers when raspberry and blueberry beers were all the rage? From the big brewers, dry beers and ice beers exploded into massive popularity and then died a very quick death. There was one point in the mid-1990s when red beers seemed poised to take over the brewing world. IPA showed a similar growth pattern, taking off in the 1990s and early 2000s to become the most popular craft-brewed style. But there are some key differences between what has happened with IPA and what happened to those other beer styles that burned out so quickly.

IPA has been the most popular beer style competing in the Great American Beer Festival® competition year after year. This hasn't changed in the 20 years or so that entry number records have been made available, and IPA shows no signs of being supplanted by any other style. Brewers like brewing the IPA style, they like drinking IPAs, and they love hops. Now the beer drinking public has embraced hops in a big way. It is important to recognize that IPA is driven by hop flavor, because, with all the hop breeding and research that is currently being done, brewers will continually be able to evolve and refine the IPA style and their own IPA flavors. There's only so much a brewer can do with a red ale, but the IPA style provides an almost limitless canvas with which to work, and that lends a lot to its sustainability as the world's most popular craft beer style. In recent years, I have been privileged to evaluate, sample, and test brew with some amazing experimental hops that are being developed. These hops have a wide array of new and unusual flavors. I sampled hops that smelled like bubblegum, orange cream, lemon candy, key lime, strawberries, and even bourbon barrel flavors full of vanillin and coconut qualities. Once these experimental hops are released, I imagine they will lend their flavors to a new wave of IPA that is sure to come. Combining these new hop flavors with other exotic culinary ingredients will lead to more imaginative IPAs. The possibilities are endless.

When I published my book, *IPA: Brewing Techniques, Recipes and the Evolution of India Pale Ale*, in 2012, I knew several things in the book would likely be out of date very soon after I wrote it. Mistakenly though, I predicted that the new knowledge would come from historical research on the real origins of the IPA style. I knew so many talented and passionate brewing historians that were really diving into the history of IPA that I figured more game-changing details would quickly be forthcoming. Instead, what has happened is that IPA has branched off into many substyles, many more than I could have ever predicted. As little as seven years ago, who would have known that citrus-infused IPAs, coffee IPAs, chocolate IPAs, Brett IPAs, and other IPAs combined with exotic foods and botanicals would have taken off to the extent that they have? And who could have dreamed up the popularity of hazy, juicy, and softly bittered New England IPA, a subset of the IPA style that is brewed so contrary to most seasoned brewers' IPA brewing techniques that it has become one of the most controversial styles out there? It is so different than almost any IPA that has come before it with one very important exception, the New England IPA is massively hoppy in aroma and taste, like an IPA should be. It is proving itself to be a real thing, and not just a fad. IPAs are here to stay, and brewers, being curious, experimental, and risk takers, will continue to explore new flavor combinations with new hop varieties and will continue to try new and unconventional techniques to make their hoppy beer stand out from the crowd.

I cannot think of anyone more suited to documenting this emerging path of IPA than Dick Cantwell. Dick has been a tireless champion in the world of craft beer since he started brewing in Seattle in the early 1990s. After stints at a few local breweries, including Pike Brewing (which may have been where I first met him), Dick helped start Elysian Brewing in Seattle and became a national craft beer icon. There he brewed great IPAs like Space Dust IPA and the incredible Avatar Jasmine IPA that very much foretold the creation of this book. Dick co-authored the excellent Brewers Publications books, *Barley Wine: History, Brewing Techniques, Recipes* with Fal Allen, and *Wood & Beer: A Brewer's Guide* with Peter Bouckaert. Dick also wrote *The Brewers Association's Guide to Starting Your Own Brewery,* helping new brewers to thoughtfully plan their own journey in brewing. He's a fantastic, engaging writer and is so well versed in beer styles and brewing techniques that he's a natural for this subject. He has served tirelessly on the board and in various other positions with the Brewers Association for many years. Very few brewers in this business are more closely aligned with what craft beer is all about than Dick Cantwell.

I remember running into Dick at John Harris' Ecliptic Brewing in Portland on the day he announced he was leaving Elysian. Dick indicated that he had a few projects in the works to fill out the duration of his required non-compete agreement with Anheuser-Busch InBev, and I am glad this book was one of them. I was excited at the chance to pre-read a copy of this book, in which Dick explores flavor combinations in IPA that few brewers could ever conceive. It's a fun and inspiring read, ripe with possibilities for all brewers. If you want to learn more about how various oils and terpenes found in hops can also be found in many foods, how these foods can then be used in hoppy IPA to provide synergistic flavors, how wood aging can enhance the character of an IPA, and how common ingredients such as coffee, chocolate, and tea can express themselves beautifully in a hoppy beer, then this book is for you!

For the last several years, brewers and the public have been asking themselves, "What's the next big thing in craft beer?" Several contending styles have emerged, but have then hit the wall of popularity that is IPA. Berliner *weisse,* Gose, sour beers, Pilsners, and barrel-aged beers have all tried to knock IPA off the mantel and have failed. I remember several years ago someone prophesized that IPA will be the next American lager, becoming the dominant beer style in American beer for a long time. That thought scared me at first, because American lager represents the worst of the bland homogeneity that characterized American beer for many decades in the twentieth century. But the more I think about this concept, the more it excites me, because IPA represents the ultimate use of hops in beer. And new hop varieties with exciting flavors are coming quickly with the resurrection and creation of many hop breeding programs. Ambitious, creative brewers are continually finding new ingredients to add to beer to combine with this ever-changing array of hop flavors. So, if IPA remains the most popular craft beer style for the foreseeable future, it means myriad new and exciting flavors will continue to be in all our beer glasses, and that's a wonderful thing.

Mitch Steele
Author of *IPA: Brewing Techniques, Recipes and the Evolution of India Pale Ale* and Founder/Brewmaster of New Realm Brewing Company

ACKNOWLEDGMENTS

An awful lot of the material for this book came from collaborative effort, first with my old brew crew from Elysian Brewing, where we brewed hundreds of different beers over the years in an atmosphere of unbridled creativity. Steve Luke (now of Cloudburst Brewing in Seattle) and Kevin Watson (now of Unified Brewing, in Seattle's White Center neighborhood) were my go-to brewers there for working on new ideas, but there were many others. My new gang at Magnolia Brewing Co. in San Francisco, headed by Seth Wile and Andrew Combs and including founder Dave McLean, are already great collaborators (or maybe they're still just being nice). Then there's my rotating crew of friendly consultants, who throughout my career have reacted honestly and with general favor; most importantly they are always on hand to brainstorm and scheme—Fal Allen, Jason Parker, Will Meyers, Ron Jeffries, and many other usual suspects. The family at New Belgium Brewing Company also figures prominently in all of this: Peter Bouckaert (now on to Purpose Brewing & Cellars in Fort Collins), Grady Hull, Ross Koenigs, Lauren Limbach, Eric Salazar, Ted Peterson, Cody Reif, Dave Glor, and anyone else who over the years has figured out how to do some of the stuff I've suggested on a larger scale.

Special mention, before we leave New Belgium, should go to Lindsay Barr, my secret technical weapon and editor; she and Mitch Steele provided excellent guidance, restraint, and suggestion. Kristi Switzer of Brewers Publications was patient, indulgent, and helpful. A lot of other breweries, businesses, and other entities pitched in as well (sometimes without knowing they were doing so) with discussions and advice on recipes and specific ingredients: Colby Chandler from Ballast Point Brewing Company, Trisha Vasquez from the Herbalist in Seattle, the guys at Pasteur Street Brewing in Ho Chi Minh City, Todd Boera of Fonta Flora Brewery, Ryan Thomas of Colorado's Hop Barley and the Alers, the staff at World Spice Merchants in Seattle, the produce department at Uwajimaya in Seattle, and the bulk tea, herb, and spice department at the Rainbow Grocery in San Francisco. Another special mention goes to my sister in sourcing, Alex Leedy, who over many years has helped me find fun new stuff to brew with at New Belgium and now at her new venture, Source of Nature. And I mustn't forget the boys (and girls) from Brazil.

Of course, of course, there's Kim Jordan, also of New Belgium (but you knew that), who had to read a lot of my favorite passages, listen to my explanations of arcane reference, and sit across the table from me as I pounded away on this monograph.

WELL, HOW DID
WE GET HERE?

In the beginning, the main accomplishment of craft brewing's first practitioners was that they were making their own beer independently of the prevailing model that had brought consumers increasingly bland and uninteresting products. What exactly that early craft beer was was somewhat indeterminate, described by adjectives as simple as "pale" and "dark," or perhaps "amber" and "blonde," but even those words stretched the ken of drinkers expected to pay around one 1980 dollar a bottle for beer of often variable quality and sporadic availability. The novelty of those renegade brewers' accomplishments was a driving force in the awareness and appreciation of these consumers for craft beer, and if that wasn't enough to keep every new brewery in business, it at least served to establish the phenomenon in popular consciousness.

Eventually taxonomies arose, at first increasingly descriptive and fanciful, but soon loosely referential to recognizable styles. Charlie Papazian's *The Complete Joy of Home Brewing* (1984) was soon followed by Greg Noonan's *Brewing Lager Beer* (1986, revised in 1996) and Dave Miller's *The Complete Handbook of Home Brewing* (1988)—this second generation of American books devoted to homebrewing helped amateur brewers recognize what made a particular style of beer. At the same time, such books as Michael Jackson's *The World Guide to Beer* (1982) and Fred Eckhardt's *The Essentials of Beer Style* (1989) provided historical background and commercial precedent for brewers to study and emulate.

Another incentive for adherence to style was competition, for how else could you say your beer was better than someone else's if you didn't acknowledge earmarks within an agreed-upon range? Where for a number of years the Great American Beer Festival (GABF®), with its dozens of entries, crowned "the Best Beer in America" with a Peoples' Choice kind of award and called it good, it soon became necessary to parse more finely, and to recognize that world beer culture might have a lesson or two even for the free spirits putting their beer in kegs and bottles in converted bicycle shops and repurposed mills and warehouses in America. Soon beers were appearing boasting Old World rubrics: Pilsner, *bock,* bitter, porter, stout, Oktoberfest, and, eventually, India pale ale (IPA). More and more styles were exhumed and emulated, often taking up the reins of stewardship dropped in their European lands of origin.

But rules, once recognized and established, were soon broken. It possibly began with the expansion or reinterpretation of a single parameter, such as alcoholic strength, perhaps the introduction of wheat or rye, or a nudge in color altering a pale precedent with chromatic license. Variations came to be creative, fanciful, in many cases stepping well outside earlier boundaries; eventually they came to be regarded as styles, or at least subcategories, in themselves, a designation often indicated by a trending increase in numbers of GABF entries. Which brings us once more to competition: not only in sanctioned and awarded quarters, but also in the jungle of professional regard and reputation, lines were crossed, bars surmounted, maximums exceeded, doubled and then tripled, the square and varicolored pane of styles came to be like so many individualized origami cranes.

This is the spirit that inspires this book, with which a single dominant style, IPA, has been turned and examined, enjoyed and pondered, and refashioned in seemingly endless variation, swapping and transposing and running in from all angles to yield hundreds, even thousands, of interesting beers. Truth be told, not every one of them is thoroughly delicious (we're experimenting, right?), but an awful lot of them are. The controlled excesses of the IPA style, bold hopping and respectable alcoholic strength, have lent themselves well to augmentation and permutation, and to interpretive and procedural evocation of kindred flavors and ingredients, to the extent that not to have at least one "eclectic" IPA in one's arsenal is to go into battle practically unarmed. For these days it is feeling a bit like a battle, however benign and comradely. The pressure to show up with a coal or two of original fire has come to be a requisite when forming a brand and identity. Quality is paramount, but a sense of inventiveness and adventure is what sticks in the beer drinker's memory and earns his or her loyalty.

It's a somewhat complicated terrain, this land of eclectic IPA, but it may not be what you think. To be sure, there's a great deal of inventiveness in the addition of hops, especially dry-hopping. In what form, at what temperature and stage of fermentation or maturation, and by which manual or mechanical means—how to introduce hops is sufficient subject for a monograph at least, or perhaps a series of articles covering differing techniques. But that isn't what we're here for now, aside perhaps from how it might affect additions of other ingredients. What we'll be looking at mainly are additions and treatments for IPA separate from those employed in traditional brewing. These will include fruits, vegetables, spices, herbs, and other ingredients such as coffee and chocolate. In addition (and this is where the "mainly" comes in), we'll take a look at the crafting of IPA using barrels and other wood products, as well as IPAs that are soured or otherwise extraordinarily influenced. Many will be beers you've encountered or that are similar to those you've encountered; others, I trust, will be beers you've never seen or heard of, in combinations of flavors and treatments that may inspire you to think up versions of your own or provide the springboard for a unique concept that leaps off in a whole other direction. We'll be having our own competitive dialogue, in a way, which chronicles the group quest of what can be done with IPA that is new and interesting.

One might wonder why IPA is the arena in which so many of these variables and variations are displayed. Why not pale ale or Munich *helles*; why not *saison*? In fairness, of course, plenty of experimentation is going on within these and other styles, but it may simply be that IPA these days is a dominant style (some would insist *the* dominant style) in craft brewing and even beyond. Sadly, one testament to this notion is the number of IPAs, eclectic and otherwise, now produced and marketed by the world's largest and most acquisitive brewers, having assembled their own New York Yankees or Real Madrid of high-priced performers from among former independents high-spotted by marketers. Rueful editorializing aside, while IPA seems to have the floor nowadays, it is also a style robust enough to maintain an identity as other ingredients are laid, troweled, and dumped atop its hoppy boldness and alcoholic might—or at least it should be if the beer in question is properly constructed and executed. And speaking of propriety, IPA is an immodest style itself, inviting excesses of concept and fixity on numerology beyond what demurer styles might allow.

As much as it is an examination of ideas already realized within the accommodating framework of IPA, this book is a study in recipe development. Beyond the crafting of a balanced and unadorned IPA—itself no small feat—myriad other elements will be brought to bear, with endless variations on type, treatment, and timing. Whether to add a fruit in the kettle, whirlpool, fermentor, or conditioning tank has a fundamental bearing on the contribution that fruit will make to the final beer. Fresh, frozen, pureed, juiced, concentrated, rendered to essence, or chemically replicated—what state of matter that fruit embodies also dictates the method and timing of its use. The same goes for herbs and spices, vanilla and coffee, and all the ways those flavorings can be introduced. Coffee alone, in fact, invites us to compare all the ways in which we discovered how best, how most essentially, to introduce the handiwork of our bean-roasting friends to various styles, including, nowadays, IPA. As in all styles, in fact all things, balance shall be our watchword.

It is testimony to craft brewers' collective willingness to learn that today we have so much to choose from where beer is concerned. It would have been easy to continue accepting the offerings of large national and regional brewers, bland, unchanging and unchallenging, unbroken throughout the year except perhaps by an artificially colored "bock" version of the same beer in February. Fortunately that's all in the past. Today there is so much to choose from that it is literally impossible to keep track, and nowhere is this more true than with IPA. Nonetheless, and even though simply by the passage of time we're doomed to failure, we still have to try. Here's hoping that, over the next hundred or so pages, we'll all manage to learn something.

SECTION I

IPAs THEN AND NOW

1

ORIGINS OF IPA:
THE EVOLUTION
OF THE PEACOCK

Any trainee tour guide at an American craft brewery knows the IPA origin story: during the honeyed age of the British Raj, a beer was required to slake the thirst of Her Majesty's conscripts on the Indian subcontinent. Heads were put together and inspiration ensued, yielding a beer sturdy enough to survive the long sea voyage—around the Cape of Good Hope, no less!—by the preservative means of prodigious alcoholic strength and the liberal use of hops. In addition, the beer was shipped in barrels, evoking a sense of oakiness and the image of rolling around in the ship's hold, delivering to the parched soldiers lining the docks of Calcutta not merely a beer but the figurative call of trumpets, accompanied by the descent from heaven of a cask-bearing Monty Python cutout. Or something like that. Properly turned, the story gets more than a few heads in the tour group nodding in recognition and agreement.

Except, according to people who know such things, the story isn't true. Oh sure, there are elements which check out. Beer was shipped in barrels in those days, not just to soldiers in India but all over the place. Lots of other things were shipped in barrels too, but you don't hear much about the flour, molasses, or herring that moved from one place to another in barrels. It's also true that beer shipped such distances was strong and it was hoppy by the standards of many other brewing styles. In those days, judging from brewing logs and brewers' accounts, most beer was strong, surprisingly strong, and everybody drank it. The average child, it would seem, reeled from the dining table straight to bed. Kentish and northern English hops were added liberally to the beer, partly for mitigating flavor and as an aid to clarification, but mainly, it must be owned, to keep the beer from arriving spoiled. As to the demands of the troops, aside from officers accustomed to the refinements of pale ale, their drink of choice would more likely have been porter or rum.

So you see, the story's almost entirely false, aside from there having been strong, pale, and hoppy beer called IPA sent to India in wooden casks. I for one have never quite understood the narrative distinction. After all, we can't hold the brewers of Queen Victoria's reign accountable for the reluctance of history to loosen its grip on a compelling and romantic story. Don't shoot the messenger (or the tour guide), they're just repeating what they've been told by those who have gone before them, some of them brewers, who similarly cannot be blamed for having an imperfect grasp of the historical and generally indistinct development of a style more firmly grounded today than it likely was during its supposed golden age.

For there's no mistaking that we are living in the heyday of IPA (at least according to us alive today) enjoying a style of beer that would likely be deemed undrinkable by its earlier eighteenth and nineteenth-century consumers. It would also, with its frequent cloudiness, and its fruity, herbal, sour, Belgian, or black dressings-up, be a source of incomprehension and eventual indifference. But we love it, don't we? We can't get enough of it.

All debunking aside, the beer that variously developed as IPA had its beginnings in London and Burton-on-Trent. The latter city, generally known for its hoppy beers brewed with mineral-rich water, these days has the strongest historical association with the IPA style. Various breweries over the years were contracted by the East India Company to provide beer for shipment to the subcontinent, the name "India Pale Ale" having arisen by around 1835 and at first mainly an indication of the product's destination. The mercantile ebb and flow of IPA's various producers and points of origin, along with rates of hopping and alcoholic strength over time, is ably chronicled in Mitch Steele's book *IPA* (2012). It is evident from Steele's research that with time less hoppy and robust versions of IPA were produced for domestic consumption compared with the beers still being sent to India, so I'm honestly not sure where that leaves us in the origin story. Like many other styles, it is clear that IPA did not arise as a single, fully-formed idea, but developed over the years on an empirical basis.

One thing that is consistent is that these beers were aged extensively. This was in order to give them time to fully condition and clarify prior to being loaded onto ships for a voyage often of several months, or otherwise run the risk of coming to explosive grief. This was partly in accord with the seasons of brewing, where, for example, beer brewed in October would benefit from the attemperation of cool weather during fermentation and subsequent aging through spring and summer, before being hopped once more prior to shipping. It was common for IPA to be a couple of years old before it was consumed, the total time being felt necessary for brightness and conditioning. With such time-consuming treatment, and the amounts of materials used for their production (IPAs were typically all-malt), it's no wonder these beers were expensive, often beyond the means of plebeian soldiers and civilians alike.

It's irresistible at this point to jump in and contrast these early IPAs with those we are familiar with today, which are typically drunk young in order to preserve delicate hop flavors and aromas. Indeed, the labels on bottles of the storied IPAs of the Russian River Brewery in Santa Rosa, California carry an exhortation not to age the beers, but to drink them fresh and in a proper glass. Even considering the diminution of hop character over time, however, it is perhaps reasonable to presume that preference thresholds for hops were sufficiently low in Victorian times for IPAs to seem bitter by comparison with other treatments and styles.

Furthermore, it is worth pointing out that the very imprecision with which the origin story of IPA has been handed down to us has contributed not only to the near-mystical contemporary reverence for the style, but also to the breadth of its interpretation. Modern practitioners can choose to run with this or that favored element and produce beers that may offend strict historical constructionists, but which satisfy and engage a less academically exacting audience susceptible both to stories and to delicious beer.

PERFIDIOUS ALBION:
BRITAIN KILLS THE GOLDEN (IPA) GOOSE

India pale ale enjoyed a period of popularity and growing production not only in England, but in Scotland, Canada, Australia, the United States, and even India itself. It may not have been the dominant world style, but it had legs and a significant geographical spread. All this was to end, however, or at least to be so severely compromised that the tape of adherence to style could seem to have run backward to the age of obscurity from which it first arose. Various cultural and commercial aspects contributed to the eventual evisceration of the IPA style as produced and consumed in Britain. Temperance movements, often difficult to pin down as to origin and effect, brought beers of strength to heel along with spirits and fortified wines. The Free Mash-Tun Act of 1880 pegged brewery production taxes to starting gravities and, hence, alcoholic strength, thereby leaving strong beers out in the cold. Both world wars brought rationing, further diluting the beers produced for a drinking public under siege. Cyclical economic downturns exposed the commercial vulnerabilities of many breweries and resulted in closures, bankruptcies, and consolidation. Compounding all this was the lager revolution, exported throughout the world from Germany and central Europe in the closing decades of the nineteenth century, which provided a lighter, less aggressive alternative. Beers called IPA continued to be brewed in Britain, but they were generally a shadow of what they had been, the style designation more evocative, once again, than indicative. Onward to today there are so-called IPAs produced in England that don't even top 4% alcohol by volume (ABV) or three dozen international bitterness units (IBU). But where neglect occurs, opportunity often arises.

THE LINKED RINGS: BALLANTINE IPA AND BEYOND

It's said that the three linked rings of Ballantine's logo—familiar even today to East Coast drinkers of the bottom-fermented "ale" brand now owned by Pabst Brewing Company—were inspired by the rings of settled condensation left by glasses or bottles on a tabletop. For the purposes of this book, the rings might be seen as embodying the linkage between successive ages of IPA, from the classic Burton-style beers emergent in America, to the Ballantine version of IPA beginning in 1880 and continuing into the 1990s, and onward to more modern emulations of its memory by early craft brewers and all that's developed since.

The post-Prohibition version of Ballantine IPA was brewed to the parameters of the Burton "golden age": 7.4% ABV, 60 IBU, and typically aged for a year in oaken vessels. In addition, a "special distillation" of Bullion hops was added in conditioning for dry hopping. In the ensuing decades, as Americans were led to believe that what they wanted were beers lighter and of less character than those they had previously enjoyed, the character lines of Ballantine IPA declined along with the rest. Just the same, even later versions are imprinted on the memories of many of us as more flavorful and interesting than nearly any other beer of the time. True old-timers may recall Ballantine Burton Ale, which was in the neighborhood of 11% ABV, aged for 20 years, and only given as gifts by the brewery. If Ballantine IPA is the pileated woodpecker—rare, but not uncommonly recalled—Ballantine Burton Ale is the ivory-billed, with no authenticated sighting in several decades.

It is said that Ballantine was literally inspiring, providing precedent for both Fritz Maytag of Anchor Brewing Company and Ken Grossman of Sierra Nevada Brewing Co. in the conception and crafting of, respectively, Liberty Ale and Celebration Ale, themselves inspiring mainstays of the craft industry. One other figure that appears repeatedly, Zelig-like, in the development of the Ballantine IPA clones is journeyman brewer Alan Kornhauser, who, while with Portland Brewing in Oregon in the early 1990s, made his best guess version with Woodstock Ale, itself later resuscitated as a holiday beer called Bobby Dazzler. Kornhauser spent many years working at Anchor as well, where he no doubt cultivated an intimacy with Liberty Ale. In more recent years, as an employee at Pabst, Kornhauser provided input for the re-release of the venerable antecedent Ballantine IPA. Talk about a feedback loop or, indeed, ring.

It's appropriate at this point to discuss those early American craft versions of IPA: Anchor's Liberty Ale and Sierra Nevada's Celebration Ale. They may have found inspiration in Ballantine's beer, but it was not the aim of either Liberty Ale or Celebration Ale to replicate it. In fact, they are very different from Ballantine IPA, having taken their cues from the preferences of the brewing teams that created them. Anchor's Liberty Ale made its first appearance in 1975 as a commemoration of Paul Revere's ride 200 years before, and later that same year became the first offering of Anchor's Special Holiday Ale, versions that have ever since been more associated with their creative use of spicing. Liberty Ale was deemed pretty bitter for the time, but soon came to achieve classic and benchmark status. Celebration Ale was first released around Christmastime in 1981, a more russet-hued beer very much its own thing. One might never have guessed the two beers received their imprint from a beer most people now living have never had. Another vitally important element shared by Liberty Ale and Celebration Ale is that they were among the first American beers committed to the use of Cascade hops. This was a vector-nudge that prefigured the growth of American IPAs in general, but also, in the embodiment of characters we shall later examine in detail, led to the more rarified and variously interpreted beers to which this book is devoted.

No account of American IPA is complete without homage paid to Bert Grant, erstwhile hop merchant, Scottish-Canadian brewing whiz kid, and at least co-originator of the brewpub concept in America. Grant's Yakima Brewing and Malting in Yakima, Washington produced an IPA beginning in 1983 that was likely the first craft-produced and packaged beer with that style designation. For anyone who knew Bert, it isn't difficult to believe that he would never have claimed inspiration from anything other than his own sensibilities.

With these antecedents springing up on the West Coast, it isn't surprising that many home and professional brewers from that time and place would take note of Anchor, Sierra Nevada, and Grant's and come up with IPAs of their own for craft brewing's next wave. I am particularly struck by members of the San Francisco Bay Area's San Andreas Malts homebrewing club of the late 1980s who created a corresponding group of beers often mentioned as early and aggressive examples of the American IPA style, and bringing them to a public disinclined to look back. Teri Fahrendorf's Bombay Bomber, once she got to Steelhead Brewing in Eugene, Oregon; Grant Johnston's Marin IPA from Marin Brewing in Larkspur, California; Ed Tringali's Bhagwan's Best from Big Time Brewery and Alehouse in Seattle, Washington; and Phil Moeller's Rubicon IPA from Rubicon Brewing in Sacramento, California—all number as early and influential examples of the style originated by former members of the San Andreas Malts. All, of course, were habitués of the Anchor tasting room and friends to early Anchor brewers Mark Carpenter and Bruce Josephs. Each in turn inspired their friends throughout California, Oregon, and Washington as the style, then barely extant in Britain, sprang up as from so many dragon's teeth to perpetuate and transform IPA into recognition and beyond.

CELL DIVISION: THE PROLIFERATION OF AMERICAN IPA

As the culture of IPA spread across the USA, one could track each successive wave through the 1990s as brewers moved from job to job and brought their West Coast sensibilities east (and vice versa), trying new hop varieties and combinations, new techniques for dry hopping, and whatever other tricks that occurred to them. The result was the production of strong, pale, and hoppy beers that now embody what the IPA style has come to be. While it's important to know approximately how and in what order things happened, we are not here to settle historical or even procedural arguments, but to understand the background for a single modern beer style that would expand into many modern styles (or perhaps substyles) offering unfettered license to craft brewers throughout the world. Many of these—we'll call them styles—have since entered the lexicon of beer enthusiasts. Before we move on, some of these styles must be mentioned, if only so that we can be mindful of the foundations upon which so much has since been built.

First and foremost among them is imperial, or double, IPA, arising from a couple of West Coast sources: Rogue Brewing in Newport, Oregon and Blind Pig Brewery in Temecula, California. In these two spots, at around the same time, it occurred to Rogue's John Maier and Blind Pig's Vinnie Cilurzo to do

IPA one better, or perhaps simply stronger and hoppier. In any case, crafting a double IPA is not as easy as it may seem; just adding more of everything will certainly amplify the essence of what makes an IPA an IPA, but presuming deliciousness is the aim, the balance of alcohol, esters, and intense hop bitterness and aroma must be skillfully tended.

Second is session IPA, a lower-gravity style with which the white flag of fatigue is waved, but proudly. Different challenges come with the execution of a session IPA, where restraining alcoholic effect and palate-coating hop intensity are the main concern. The notion of a low-alcohol IPA may be seen as oxymoronic, a risk even, but as beers have trended stronger and more intense a vocal contingent has demanded something flavorful and hoppy without the slaying effect of 9 or 10 percent alcohol. The trick with session IPAs is maintaining hoppy boldness without vegetal or grainy-tasting excess, the former quality mostly influenced by the selection of hop variety and use of dry hopping, the latter by the attention given to sparging a lower-gravity wort in order not to pull husky harshness from the grain bed.

And then there are the hybrids: white IPA, black IPA, and Belgian IPA. White IPA's parents are hoppy IPA and Belgian *witbier*, joined together in a strongish, cloudy wheat IPA and giving off not just hop aroma but the spiciness of coriander, orange peel, and the like. This style actually includes elements of what we are mainly here to discuss later in this book. Black IPA started out as a joke, I think—at least I made it—challenging the popularity of the general style by producing something antithetical and giving it a nonsensical name. In any case, black IPA is with us now, also somewhat jingoistically called Cascadian dark ale, embodying the hoppy characters of more conventional IPA with a dark-colored wort designed not to bear the roastiness and chocolatey fullness of its cousin, hoppy porter. Belgian IPA, somewhat confusingly, can be a couple of things: a strong, Belgian-style pale ale hopped to within IPA recognition; or an IPA by all measures aside from having been fermented with a Belgian yeast. No one said this was going to be easy; it just seemed that way when we were all getting started.

These days, of course, cloudy, juicy, and fruity-tasting IPAs are all the rage. It is often somewhat difficult to tell whether actual fruit is involved in the creation of some of these IPAs, or whether the effect is due to the use of distinctively fruity hops. And then, perversely, the brewers of these beers will sometimes issue one-off versions using actual fruit. They may in some circles be tagged with a New England moniker-of-origin, but like the double IPAs once loudly claimed by San Diegans and the black IPAs staked out by a tiny Northwest splinter group, they are now to be found across the United States and even beyond.

As with white IPA mentioned earlier, these beers have taken steps toward what we are here to examine in the chapters that follow. I bring them up here to provide antecedent possibility for the use of some of the ingredients in what we will call "eclectic IPA." They may turn up in our examinations of ingredients and treatments in the reflection on and search for newer, more idiosyncratic IPAs; it's also possible that they won't, leaving that kind of conceptualizing up to you. For, after all, it's you, all of you, who have made this eclectic thing happen.

WHERE IT ALL WENT FROM THERE, AND WHERE WE'RE GOING

New Belgium's former brewmaster Peter Bouckaert has never been one to get hung up on style. Perhaps this is simply because he is Belgian. Or, as the master-mind behind some of the world's most unique beers—from his own brewpub in Harelbeke, West Flanders; at Rodenbach brewery (in Roeselare, West Flanders), where he served as brewmaster and worked for nearly ten years; at New Belgium in Fort Collins, Colorado, where he pioneered the use of dozens of unique ingredients during his 21 years there; and presumably at his new gig at Purpose Brewing and Cellars, also in Fort Collins—perhaps Bouckaert believes that to impose strict adherence to style is to hamper the creative aspect of brewing. I've heard him decry the laborious parsing of style by competitions like the GABF, wanting to do away with such classification entirely. He's expressed the wistful (and possibly impish) desire to submit any entries with which he is associated as "American Pale Ale." After all, he maintains, that's what they are.

Well, that's a bit like where we are with all these beers that we're about to take a look at. Some might be considered fruit or vegetable beers; others, if entered for judgement, may likely turn up in an herb and spice category. Still others perhaps embrace overarching coffee or chocolate flavors; at the very least, if such elements are perceptible, then not to put them in the coffee or chocolate category might be to invite rejection out of hand. An IPA aged in wood, particularly wood little enough used that it imparts some of its character to the finished beer, had better own up to being a wood-aged beer. Ditto for IPAs exhibiting the influence of *Lactobacillus* or *Brettanomyces*: unless such determination is signaled by categorization, a judge, or a customer, is likely to think they are tasting a beer where something went terribly wrong.

So perhaps, like Bouckaert's myriad American pale ales, these beers are all simply American IPA. That's what they are, after all, however they are made and whether they happen to have been brewed in California, Florida, or Michigan, or crafted in Ho Chi Minh City by a brewer from Oregon. It is to be hoped, even demanded, that they have enough in common with the basics of modern IPA to be recognizable as such beneath the layering of balanced interpretation, and that such treatment provides joyful and delicious interplay between the essence of IPA and the creative and considered touch given them by brewerly inspiration. American IPA. That's what they are.

Now before we go on with our discussion of hops and all they have meant to the development of IPA, a word should perhaps also be said on behalf of malt and the important part it plays in the balance of all beers, even American IPA. Most modern American IPAs are fairly pale, making use of American malts more neutral in flavor than the sturdier-flavored English varieties of yore. This doesn't mean that malt should be an afterthought. There are those who believe that IPAs are entirely about hops, and in some cases literally that there is no such thing as too bitter or hoppy a beer. (I'll let that one just stand there in its absurdity.) All successful beers are about balance, and to play down the contribution of malt, even for a beer style known for its hops, is to go into our examination one-eyed. Come to think of it, maybe that's the idea.

THE SUBTLE, AND NOT SO SUBTLE, MACHINERY OF HOPS

Once upon a time, throughout most of brewing's history, hops were a simple machine. Like a lever, an inclined plane, or a wheel, hops had a pretty uncompli-cated job to do. On a purely practical basis, hops helped preserve beer beyond what other spice mixtures could; that's one big reason they came into general use. In the matter of ingredients, hops offered mitigating bitterness to the sweet-ness of malt, along with incidental flavor and a bit of aroma. In old recipe books and brewers logs hops were not distinguished by variety, and any difference among them was mainly denoted by geographical origin, for example, East Kent or Hallertau. Sometimes a practical fact, such as harvest time, was included as part of the name, like Mittelfrüh, which roughly translates as "middling early." Most early recipes just listed hops, and, of course, these hops would come from nearby where the beer was brewed. Where else would they have come from?

Over time differences in characteristics were noted between the hops of one place and those of another, and varieties came to be designated as the agricultural arts and sciences developed. By the time the American hop industry had become established in Washington and Oregon variety awareness was well developed, but the preferences of brewers were limited to a few stalwarts. Disease was an intermittent issue, with whole crops that concentrated on single varieties being particularly susceptible to molds and pests. Diversification made good sense, and research was ongoing for new varieties that might prove hardier and more resistant to these phenomena.

One variety that made its appearance in the late 1960s was Cascade (though it hadn't yet been given that name). Resistant to the downy mildew that sometimes plagued other varieties, Cascade was also noted by its adherents to have an interesting fresh aroma, which at first proved too distinctive for most brewers. Eventually, however, some came around. Coors Brewing Company, to its credit, was one, and Anchor Brewing Company was another. As noted in the previous chapter, Anchor made use of the new Cascade in its Liberty Ale, so not only was Liberty Ale arguably the first IPA produced by the embryonic craft brewing industry, it was one of the very first beers in America to use the Cascade hop. Along with Sierra Nevada's use of it in its Pale Ale (and other beers), Cascade quickly became the differentiating hop that emergent craft brewers simply had to have.

Where other, more traditional hop varieties were described with words connoting mustiness and decay, such as barnyard or grassy (which, somewhat paradoxically, often meant pretty much the same thing), or here and there as being lightly spicy or floral, descriptions of Cascade suggested fruit, citrus fruit in particular; grapefruit has frequently been evoked. I've always considered it more orangey, and we may as well acknowledge the rampant subjectivity where hop evaluation is concerned. One person's bright and lively is another's onion and garlic. But back then Cascade was a whole new thing where hops were concerned. Its bitterness quotient was middling to somewhat high when compared with European varieties long in use, even those cultivated in America, which made it relatively economical for bittering. But it was as a late-use hop that Cascade showed itself best. As American craft brewers revived (and overdid) flavor and aroma hopping, and as they developed techniques for dry hopping finished, or nearly finished, beer, they created beers unlike practically anything that had come before. Cascade remains far and away the most popular hop used in craft brewing, and it has held that spot for many years.

Lupulin Lines

When I was in high school I worked for a summer hoeing fields and pollinating corn at a seed research farm several miles outside of the town in southern Minnesota where my family lived. The work was tedious and full of lots of circuitous conversation, the soundtrack the endlessly repeated AM radio playlist of the day; we weren't exactly entrusted with high-level decision-making where the invention of new plant hybrids was concerned. At the end of each day, however, we were allowed to roam the experimental rows and take home as much corn as we wanted, since the relevant information had already been noted and the crop itself served no further experimental use. Some of the plants were enormously tall with little tiny ears, others short with ears dragging them down toward the ground. Some ears were crammed with maloccluded kernels of irregular size, others hardly formed kernels at all. Enough of them were just right to allow us to fill our bags and take them home to the family table.

The breeding and hybridization of hops results in a similar mix, I'd guess, of characteristics useful and odd, with now and then a variety rising to the breeder's notice with its commercial possibilities. There seems a certain inevitability to the way modern hops have worked out, with so many varieties these days tickling the fancies of inventive brewers, but a lot of what we've come to take for granted may never have come to pass.

Take Cascade. The offspring of good old Fuggle and another Fuggle-type with the intriguing first name of Serebrianka, Cascade was bred primarily for disease resistance, but it became, with a certain amount of patronage and happenstance, the perennially most-used hop in craft brewing. Given what little most of us know about crop husbandry, it might seem that the people involved in conducting such experimentation would have combined Cascade, once it proved itself a keeper, with just about everything else in the hope that a sturdy and engaging lineage would yield a whole clan of related hops in the Cascade mold. It's true that there are Cascade offspring out there, and some of them can be found on the shelves in many of our cold rooms. Crystal, Delta, Sterling, Mandarina—all are progeny of Cascade, but none of them, with all due respect, are exactly setting the brewing world on fire. Mandarina probably garners the most enthusiasm among the group. The fact is that breeding is hard and yields a pretty low return. And it takes time. Often a decade passes before any gleam of inspiration or permutation makes it to the blue-papered sample bricks on the tables of hop brokers at the Craft Brewers Conference.

Where today's popular varieties are concerned, another story worth telling centers on Centennial, the craft industry's second-most popular variety these days behind Cascade. Like Cascade, Centennial captured the fancy of craft brewers eager for a different and compelling aroma when it was released around 1990. It came under fire within hops' governing bodies because of general indifference by the larger brewers, who also footed the bill for these and other research activities. Ordered to destroy all evidence and existence of a variety only seeming to have relevance for upstart and penurious craft brewers, hop industry stalwart and craft brewing advocate Ralph Olson almost single-handedly kept Centennial going, giving it an alias-number and making it available as though it were an entirely new hop. I well remember CFJ-90, its initials given by three co-conspirators; eventually, it was to be given its more august moniker.

The mid-1990s saw the arrival of Amarillo, a variety developed and exclusively controlled by Virgil Gamache Farms, Inc. Today many hop varieties are being generated by private and relatively secretive arrangements, with rights and restrictions disbursed by the families and consortiums that bring them about. Where once one could simply consult the public USDA list of origins and specifications, these days new hops arise from the mists, often pre-named and pre-marketed. Hence, family trees of the hops that today everybody wants to have are not so easily perused. Variety-specific caps, T-shirts, and water bottles are more easily procured, as growers and brokers chase the brass ring of fashion.

Within individual varieties, whatever their origin, the geographical provenance of specific lots of hops is an enormously important differentiator. This is what everybody shows up for every fall in Yakima and on farms in Oregon and Idaho: to pick the stuff they really like and to get the jump on less attentive and committed brewers. Statistics on harvest times and kilning temperatures have also become part of the story behind any given batch of hops used to craft the hoppy and eclectic beers we have all come to love. Who knew there would be so many choices to make, so many elements to enhance and pick a preference for when masterminding our creations?

One further note in the Favorite Hops Ever Department. Steve Dresler, recently retired from his long gig at Sierra Nevada, and one of the most knowledgeable and engaged hopheads on the brewing side of the industry, recalls a hop he once encountered—loved, he says, above all others— but which in the shell game of experimental variety numbers and fleeting availability lost track of and never found again. But history, all histories, need these unrealized dreams to keep us all wistful and wondering.

As the eighties unspooled and the nineties followed, other fruity and distinctive hops made their way into the craft market and came into common use. Chinook made its appearance in 1985, offering higher alpha-acid "oomph" than Cascade, with a distinctive grapefruit flavor and aroma that many found carried through even when used primarily for bittering. Centennial was released five years later. It too provided higher levels of alpha acid, with aroma attributes described on the current Yakima Chief–Hopunion (YCH) website as "lemon and floral."[1] I often noted a comforting strawberry jam bloom of aroma on adding Centennial to the kettle. Descriptors run rampant on the YCH web page for Amarillo, a proprietary variety produced by Virgil Gamache Farms, Inc. and first arriving in the mid-1990s: grapefruit, orange, lemon, melon, apricot, and peach.[2]

Clearly, aspirations of fruitiness were becoming increasingly important for brewers, who began to pay closer attention to oil-derived compounds, chemically classed as terpenes, in hop analysis as markers for particular flavors in beer. Conifers are particularly noted for their terpene character (think of turpentine), but many other herbs are evoked in the descriptions and definitions of terpenes and terpenoids. Some commonly noted compounds sought out by craft brewers were myrcene, which suggested citrus, cannabis, and thyme; linalool, which also carried citrus along with flowers and spice; and geraniol, evocative of geranium, lemon, and rose oil. Other compounds perhaps a touch more obscure were subjectively redolent of other items from the specialty produce aisle, such as rosemary, green apple, or shiso. For the brewer willing to notice, a cornucopia of flavors and aromas were there for the experimenting. A more complete list can be found under "Terpenic Tie-ins to Hops, Fruits, Herbs and All the Rest" in the appendix.

It was spring of 2008, and I was judging the International Pale Ale category at the World Beer Cup[SM] in San Diego. One beer caught my attention so dramatically with an altogether new aroma of fruitiness for me that I jumped out of my chair and, no doubt in direct contravention of the rules, walked over to the next judging table where Peter Bouckaert of New Belgium was sitting. I asked him to taste it, and he did, along with another judge at the table, a guy from New Zealand, who nodded knowingly and said, oh yeah, that was Nelson Sauvin. With its (retrospectively) unmistakable aroma of fresh gooseberries and a name evoking white wine grapes, it was a hop unlike anything I had ever encountered.

---

[1] "A Dual Purpose Hop: Centennial, United States," YCH Hops website, under "Aroma Profile: Floral, Citrus," accessed October 26, 2017, https://ychhops.com/varieties/centennial.

[2] "An Aroma Hop: Amarillo® VGXP01 CV., United States," YCH Hops website, under "Aroma Profile: Floral, Citrus," accessed October 26, 2017, https://ychhops.com/varieties/amarillo-brand-vgxp01.

Over the next couple of years other New Zealand hops, with their exotic, Maori-sounding names—Riwaka, Motueka, Rakau, Wai-iti—and radical fruit aromas, blew the lid off an associative sensibility which to that point had seemed enclosed by Northwest evergreen forests, the citrus orchards of California's Central Valley, and perhaps the growhouses of Humboldt and Mendocino Counties in Northern California. The international race was on in the search for new and more exotically fruity aromas for use in hop-forward beers.

The Where and When of Hopping

Brewers are well aware that the timing of hopping, in the kettle, whirlpool, fermentor, or conditioning vessel (including the keg or cask), is of essential importance to the hop character and overall effect it has on any beer. I even recall the efforts of a particular brewer friend of mine several years ago who, in an effort to maximize the effect of late hopping, placed a single hop cone in each bottle of his IPA; however sound the principle may have been, the outcome was not felicitous (another brewer friend of mine, who we figured out later had judged this beer, wrote in his comments: "Bad brewer, bad!").

We know that certain hop varieties are most appropriately used for bittering. Others show their colors best (as literally demonstrated by spectroscopic examination) as later additions, where aroma compounds are kept from the destructive rigors of the boil and live on to rise from the glass. The same could be said of many of the ingredients addressed in this book, and an effort has been made in the tables that accompany chapters 3, 4, and 5 to suggest the effects depending on the various points of use. That said, a few basic considerations ought to be made when deciding when and in what combination hops are added to the process when brewing these many-layered beers.

Once you know a bit about the flavor-active compounds found in the essential oils of hops, it's worth recognizing that certain ones will not perceptibly survive the heat and activity of the boil, whereas others will undergo biotransformation during fermentation. Dry hopping or the use of oils can provide the compelling kiss that best combines the hop character with the additional ingredients of your eclectic IPA. Furthermore, the flavors and aromas unlocked by a late hot-side addition (in the whirlpool, for example), along with nominal attendant bitterness, can be just the thing when crafting any IPA, and can provide escort to steeped teas, herbs, and the other materials of broader invention.

Several years ago dry hopping was usually only briefly referenced, an afterthought of a pound or two added to the fermentor at knockout or a bag hastily stuffed and secured by a keg's bung. Today, as we all know, it's become something of a vertical industry, with not only hop varieties and specific hop products identified as particularly prized for late cold-side additions, but specialized equipment of varying design available to the committed dry hopper. It is really this attention—one might even call it obsession—which has allowed nuances of flavor and aroma resident in hops to be unlocked, free to combine with the essential elements of fruits, herbs, and all the rest, that justifies the development of these hybrid beers. It is partly conceptual, perhaps dictated by geographic or cultural association. It is partly chemical, the makeup of a particular hop variety and how it is deconstructed by the sensibilities of the brewer and the palate of the beer drinker. And it is partly combinational, the layering that takes place not just from the contribution of hops, but from the combination of hops with other ingredients. There is a lot, in short, to think about when deciding when to add which hop to an eclectic IPA.

Practically speaking, it can be useful to combine various elements roughly in proportion, just to see if what you're thinking about is something you like. A dollop of this and a sprig of that, possibly cold and possibly steeped, can give you some idea of how things will play. You might also try rubbing a pinch of hop pellets with whatever other dry materials you're considering. Or there's adding a dash of a particular juice mix or zested peel to a glass of finished beer. Try adding an herb under review to hot and cold liquid, to wort or beer, at any stage in the process to get a sort of unscientific and subjective preview of where the considered material should be added. Some stalwarts do well on the hot side, as we've outlined; others grudgingly unfold in fermentation, conditioning, or later, much the same way hops do.

DIM THE LIGHTS: THE EVOCATIVE BECOMES ACTUAL

From an apparent industry-wide obsession with fruity hop flavors and aromas, replete with the hemispherical counterpoint of the Pacific Northwest and Australia and New Zealand, it wasn't much of a conceptual stretch for hoppy beers, IPAs in particular, to begin appearing augmenting evocative effects with actual fruit. On the surface, the use of various fruits should be obvious and associative: citrus fruits such as orange, grapefruit, lemon, lime, and more unusual types such as yuzu, combined with the likes of Chinook, Cascade, Amarillo, Mosaic, and other hops often described as "citrusy"; fruits such as berries, peaches, plums, cherries, even mangoes and melons, added to beers brewed with diversely fruity hop varieties such as many of those from the Southern Hemisphere; and tropical fruits such as pineapple, passion fruit, lychee, and coconut added to beers using hops evoking those flavors, wherever they come from. But while association is relatively easy—despite, one has to think, the wishful, downright speculative descriptions by hop merchants of flavors and aromas unheard of even a couple of decades ago—counterpoint requires the inspiration and skill of the accomplished chef or brewhouse recipe crafter.

Think of making pies. Berries are good by themselves or in combination with each other. Rhubarb is good, and traditional, with strawberry. But think about adding dates to an apple pie, which itself is often augmented with cinnamon and other spice, as is peach, as are a lot of things, and you begin to get the idea that pineapple and lemon are not so bad together, or kumquat and melon—or even cucumber. Each of these fruits, each of these additional flavors, carries within it a balance of bitterness, sweetness, tartness, and other elements that can ally with the taster's expectations or act in delicious contravention to them. That is the secret to both the sensual and intellectual appreciation of tasting . . . well, anything.

We shouldn't yet leave the subject of fruit without some discussion of esters. A result of the process of fermentation, esters in beer are combinations of alcohol and organic acids, both of which can be represented by many types, brought together by yeast enzymes to create fruity flavors and aromas. The most obvious one, and the one which leads any discussion of esters, is isoamyl acetate, which is most readily identifiable as the "banana" in southern German-style *hefeweizen* (it is the traditional Bavarian yeast used in hefeweizen that produces this effect). Another common ester is ethyl acetate, which can be lightly pearlike in low concentrations, but becomes harsher and more solventlike when more is present. Other esters can remind one of apples and peaches, and sometimes more unpleasantly of raw pumpkin (this can be a marker of acetaldehyde). Esters can be delicious flavor enhancers in beers where such flavors are appropriate, but should probably be avoided in cleaner tasting, less fruity beers. Lagers, for example, are traditionally considered to be better if fermentation esters are absent to minimal. Since fermentation temperature is roughly proportional to ester production, the lower temperatures used when executing lagers are generally self-policing where esters are concerned, if properly managed. Ester production can also be tied to yeast growth, with (perhaps paradoxically) higher rates of growth generating a less pronounced ester character.

As observed, yeasts derived from geographically distinct regions produce beers of appropriate fruitiness due to the esters produced in the normal course of fermentation. The secret to the subtle, fruity flavors and aromas in otherwise lightweight English-style bitters and pale ales is due to the management of ester production, attributable mainly to yeast selection; less desirably, these yeasts can also produce excessive amounts of buttery diacetyl. Such factors as fermentation temperature, oxygenation, pitching rate, and even vessel geometry can play a part, each element of which can be tinkered with to alter the degree of ester contribution. The pressure, or its lack, under which fermentations are conducted can also affect the rate of ester generation, with the open squares of traditional English brewers contributing to the characteristic fruitiness of their beers.

Esters can be fleeting as well. You won't find much about this in the scientific literature, because such things as ester production are generally presented as absolute, but anyone who has tasted the lovely peachiness in a barleywine or other strong ale in progress and noticed, dishearteningly, that quality fading as fermentation advances knows what I'm talking about. Well, maybe the solution is to add peaches (or mangoes, or something else) to the beer at a later stage, to build back in the best of what has already occurred but since faded. Maybe, and maybe not—success using this method is not guaranteed. It should also be noted that a properly managed fermentation will include a "diacetyl rest," a period of slightly elevated temperature built in to allow the reduction of this least pleasant of esters. In any case, esters are very real contributors to the flavor and balance of many IPAs, and can be brought into the equation when contemplating the addition of some other ingredient.

So far, we have mainly considered fruit as an appropriate extension or augmentation of the flavors evident in conventionally produced IPAs and other beers (we may as well acknowledge that other beers exist). We know vegetables are good for us—but are they good in beer? While perhaps less flashy, less broad-brushed and aggressive, they too can contribute to beers of distinction and inventiveness. Fruits would seem a natural, of course, for all the reasons and examples outlined above. In addition, fruits are sweet. The sugars they contribute to beer can become integrated in mashing and in fermentation, though be advised that their flavors are not appreciable on the literally molecular level. If added late (ideally in a sterile state) fruit can add a measurable and duplicable amount of sweetness and flavor to finished beer. Without this degree of sweetness working for them, however, vegetables are a bit more of a challenge. We as brewers are also conditioned to avoid anything smacking of the vegetal in sensory perception. And yet . . .

Mentioning the avoidance of the vegetal brings us back to IPA. As it should. The artistry of dry hopping in the hands of a lesser master can, and often does, bring vegetal flavors to the fore. Tasting a flight of IPAs at the judging table will quickly cause to fall away those beers that use hops in less than pristine condition, have aged beyond optimal retention of aroma, or have been inadequately parted from all that green material. There is a rough corollary in contemplating the use of vegetables in making IPA: where fruits present a what-you-see-is-what-you-get aspect (you know, for example, what an apple tastes like, and hence what sorts of flavors it might bring to a beer), vegetables generally require some sort of synthesis to be integrated effectively. Consider the fact that in most cases we cook vegetables to soften them and to make their sugars accessible for greater tastiness. Fruits too can be cooked, of course, and vegetables eaten raw (though sometimes, it's tempting to say, to prove a point), but when considering using vegetables to make IPA, one needs to think a move or two ahead to realize the appropriateness (or delicious inappropriateness) of many vegetables. We'll get more into the different stages of hands-on processing of these things later in chapter 3. But unlike the use of fruit in IPA, where we consider the fruit-like contributions of the hop varieties we've chosen, with vegetables we are more likely to think ahead to the accent or aspect that lurks somewhere close to the indefinable core of the beer we are trying to make. We will, first and foremost, be pragmatic and consider deliciousness above the conceptual design when using vegetable ingredients in an augmented IPA, but for the sake of getting into the idea, think about a couple of examples: the sugary depth of roasted carrots or sweet peppers cohabiting the heart of a double IPA; the right balance of astringency and variety-specific flavor of squash or pumpkin in a seasonal IPA, and with the appropriate, perhaps earthier or spicier, hops; the bright and peppery accent of cucumber or celery (neither of them cooked, no, never cooked) in a lighter session IPA. What do you think of that? Well, I'm not sure either, but we'll think about it as we go along.

While using vegetables in an IPA might be considered a stretch—it's more contrapuntal than harmonic, to be sure—adding herbs and spices to beers already showing aspects of some of these flavors in their hop-derived character is nearly as familiar as donning that holey and arm-stretched hoody you saved from your first brewing job all those years ago. Herbs and spices are certainly traditional, for those who care about that. (Remember *gruit*, remember witchcraft, remember Charlie Papazian's spiced holiday ale?) The fact is, those terpenes in hop essential oils that we mentioned several pages back—the ones acquiring more and more descriptors over the years like the feathers and jewels on Bartholomew Cubbins's hats—draw herbal and spicy comparisons alongside the fruity ones. It's therefore highly appropriate to consider adding herbs and spices to hoppy beers like IPA.

What is an herb? What is a spice? Is tea an herb? Is chili pepper a spice? Fortunately, this book is more about ideas than taxonomy, but still, these are the kinds of questions that plague us as we obsessively seek to move forward. Dictionarily speaking, spice is an aromatic vegetable product used to season or flavor foods; the *Oxford English Dictionary* (second edition, 1989) confers an additional, tropical connotation as to origin, as well as mentioning vaguely inherent, vaguely occurrent preservative qualities. Botanically, herbs come from plants that do not produce woody tissue and instead die down to the ground after producing the leaves and stems that are used by resourceful druids (like us) for their medicinal, savory, or aromatic qualities. A quick reading of these definitions shows that herbs and spices are prized for their general aromatic quality and associated flavor. Tea plants, since we're on the subject, take a number of years to produce leaves suitable for subsequent drying, fermentation, steeping, and sipping, and so technically no, tea is not an herb, but since many "teas" are in fact dried herbal mixtures we'll be considering their use both in the chapter covering herbs and in the one covering coffee and chocolate. And no, since you've brought it up, chili pepper is not a spice, it's technically a fruit, at least when fresh or roasted. Since dried and powdered chilies are used in the same way as spices, a pinch here, a particular measure there, they are a bit of a hybrid where flavoring treatments are concerned. As long as chilies make it into IPA, when and where and in whatever quantity you want, let's not stress too much about where it is they actually belong.

More than most other styles of beer, IPA lends itself well to herbal treatment. Rosemary, thyme, basil, shiso, juniper, and spruce—these are the stuff of the brewer's lazy strut, beguiling accents for the substantial beers we're talking about. But wait. Juniper and spruce? Those are evergreens. I get the terpene connection, but are evergreens an herb? Ask your mother. Spices, on the other hand, must be carefully chosen: peppercorns yes, cinnamon and allspice probably no. That said, I'm not the one coming up with the new and fabulous IPAs you are destined to make, so go ahead, prove me wrong. But why not some of the spices (aside from cinnamon, that is) we associate with curry, for instance, turmeric or cardamom? Let's just say you'll need a subjectively certifiable reason (such as deliciousness) to put them in a boldly hoppy beer of malty fortitude.

Similarly challenging, perhaps, the addition of coffee, chocolate, or vanilla to IPAs (which is happening more and more) is something that must show up in such a way that the result is eye-opening and engagingly tasty. It isn't completely surprising, given the artisanal congruence of craft beer, small-batch coffee roasting, and chocolate manufacture in the United States over the past few decades, that such things would find their way into beer. The association, however, is most often with beers that resemble the color of the products involved, stouts and porters in particular. But origins, roasts, and treatments of coffee vary as widely as the world and its tattooed roasters, giving us new ways to introduce fruitiness and acidity to an IPA already showing elements of either one, or perhaps both. Chocolate too can become part of a pale and hoppy beer, perhaps its bitterness combining with well-chosen hopping in a beguiling way. Vanilla, well, a little of that goes a long way in anything; that's one reason it's often sold as a single bean or as an alcoholic extraction. But vanilla has to be considered, because it's so often combined with chocolate. In fact, chocolate often travels with a plus-one, at various times bringing along chilies, cinnamon, or orange, for example, most often in a dark beer. But who knows? We're all about straining credulity, right?

WOOD-AGED AND SOUR IPAs

The Long and One-Eyed Lens of History

It's well known, even if imperfectly, that during its first golden age IPA was shipped to India and elsewhere around the world in wooden barrels. Combine this with the fact that these days something like 85% of all American brewers are using or experimenting with treatments of wood in beer, and the occurrence of wood- and barrel-aged IPAs is not only unsurprising, but inevitable. The surprising thing, to my mind, is that there aren't more of them. Wood-aged beers entered for judging in competitions are still dominated by dark entries. A large part of this is probably because bourbon barrels are the easiest and cheapest to get one's hands on and any residual liquor combines best with porters, stouts, and dark Scottish ales (it may also be partly due to the early days of barrel aging in craft brewing, when the "wow" factor threshold for dark beers was astonishingly low). While many of these beers are phenomenally delicious, we are not here to talk about them.

The first IPA I had a professional hand in was at the Pike Place Brewery in Seattle (now known as the Pike Brewing Company) in about 1992. Having received special dispensation from owner Charles Finkel to use American hops in the beer, we chose Chinook (Cascade remained taboo, in Charles's mind harsh and redolent of the competition) and combined it with more traditional East Kent Goldings and, probably, Fuggle. The yeast we used, the yeast we always used, was an indeterminately mutated strain that had once been Fuller's, so check there as well. In addition, and ticking a further conceptual box, we hung a bag of Limousin oak chips in the conditioning tank for a week's contact. The beer was instantly popular, but annoyingly some drinkers perceived the nominal furfural contribution (a woody butterscotch flavor) of the oak as diacetyl. Aargh!

But how times have changed. These days, the genuflection toward Brittanic antecedent has been reduced to the half-turned nod of the casual worshipper. We know the original IPAs were brewed with East Kent Goldings; we know they were brewed with fruity (and often diacetyl-ridden) English yeasts; we know (or we think we know) that they traveled to India. But we don't have to do any of that. We can use American hops, New Zealand hops; we can ferment them with attenuative and relatively neutral American yeasts; we can still give them names semi-literately referential to the Raj; we can do whatever we want. Just the same, we are fascinated by wood, and these days can mainly trust our customers to recognize its contribution. We'll talk later in chapter 6 about the best ways, and the many ways, to produce IPAs in wood and with wood.

Partly because of the historic association with time spent in transit on all those putative sea voyages, but mainly because these days brewers are whacking everything in sight with the sour stick, IPAs wood-aged and otherwise are once again appearing with some kind of sour treatment. We'll get more into the whys and hows in chapter 6, but right off the bat this combination of hoppy and sour is not easy to execute due to hop bitterness hampering the actions of certain souring microorganisms. Ah, but there's always dry hopping, isn't there? Oh, uh, Spoiler Alert! (I guess I should have said that first.) In any case, brewers are finding the flavor contributions in fermentations that use lactobacilli, pediococci, and *Brettanomyces* an interesting challenge when producing beers that still (mostly) qualify as IPA.

Before we move onto a more analytical and practical presentation of each of these categories of augmented, or eclectic, IPA, it ought to be noted in closing here that in terms of strict classification each of these eclectic IPAs would likely not fall within any judging category that primarily designates IPA. Fruited IPAs? Fruit beer. An IPA made with tea or flowers? Herb and spice. A beer such as Stone Brewing's Enjoy By 02.14.17 Chocolate & Coffee IPA? Depending on the person thinking of entering it for competition, either coffee beer or chocolate beer. Sour and/or wood-aged IPA? Same deal. Official (and perhaps not-so-official) judging of any of these beers would require that features of both parent styles be evident: sufficient alcoholic strength and both bitter and aromatic hoppiness to be recognizable and enjoyable as an IPA, augmented by the uniqueness and deliciousness of whichever other element has been bound to it. Perhaps, just to make it easier, and in the spirit of Peter Bouckaert's leveling of the demands of style guidelines, these are all just American IPA, variously conceived.

SECTION II

CRAFTING ECLECTIC IPAs

NOTES ON THE RECIPES

A certain amount of brewing knowledge is assumed in the formulation of and directions for the recipes at the end of each of the chapters that follow. Some basic assumptions are a bit slippery—the United States is a large country and there is an even wider world out there, so several important factors will vary depending on region. Local water chemistry, chiefly, but also elevation, consumer preference, and the availability and variability of the materials needed to make many of these beers—I leave it to you to make do as best you can, knowing what you do about your circumstances and capabilities.

Just the same, some observations are in order, given the fact that the basic recipes (without all the fancy stuff) aren't all that different from each other. Naturally I've tried to introduce what I think are appropriate raw ingredients to each beer, recognizing both the limitations of my own experience and the amazing array of stuff available these days. Like the rest of this book, the recipes presented are intended to spark discussion, disagreement, and improvement. If you want a more bitter beer, then by all means, put the alpha to the metal; if an ingredient you like isn't mentioned, do me the favor of its inclusion and, likely, improving the beer in question. You might even get some ideas for beers in other styles. So much of what all of us do is a dialogue. Let's make sure that, despite the various winds of change, we keep the discussion going.

Water

Even in the earliest days of IPA brewing, water chemistry differed between beers brewed in London and in Burton-on-Trent, with the latter weighing in substantially harder than the former. I won't personally hazard a generalization as to relative compatibility with rates of hopping, but different waters no doubt yield different results. I will reproduce the following paragraph from Mitch Steele's book on IPA:

> *The high calcium in Burton water reduces wort pH, which increases enzyme activity in the mash. This allows for reduced protein, better starch conversion, and drier beer. The extra calcium facilitates yeast flocculation and also provides better trub separation in the whirlpool and less protein haze in the beer. With high levels of calcium, there is less color development during the wort boil and a lower harshness in hops' bitter character. The high sulfate levels in the water give a full, yet dry flavor, enhance the hop bitterness, and produce a crisper, cleaner bitterness than beers brewed with softer water. (Steele 2012, 68)*

Well, that's IPA all over, isn't it? The water in Seattle, where I've done nearly all of my brewing, is extremely soft and, to be honest, I've done very little to tinker with the mineral makeup of my brewing liquor over the years. I recognize that greater attention to this would probably have made for beers of greater nuance and specific hop complexity. Seattle's water chemistry is certainly closer to that of London than Burton. Seattle's water is also very similar to the water in Portland (Oregon), San Francisco, the Front Range of Colorado, and western North Carolina (as well as Prague in the Czech Republic, for what that's worth). But it's very different from the water in the Midwest, or the water in much of the northeastern United States. My point is that to prescribe specific mineral additions to your brewing water would, in my view, be counterproductive and needlessly eggheaded. Take a look at the water analyses of anyplace you think makes wonderful IPA, like San Diego, Vermont, or Middleburg Heights, Ohio. While many of the brewers in those places do different things to their brewing water, the point is that terrific IPA can be made anywhere. I'm not saying don't do anything, but I am saying that to tell you exactly what to do might prove conceptually sound but practically wrong-headed. I am therefore leaving out notes for specific water treatment in the recipes, with the exception of those provided by others.

Malt

Malt may not be where IPA's main drama is played out, but its importance should not be underestimated. Most of the IPA recipes presented in this book are made with American pale base malt, augmented by various specialties that I happen to like. Some of them use English base malt; in some instances where the base beer is intended to be extra pale, in order, say, to allow some colored specialty ingredient to have full play, the recipe uses Pilsner malt. You'll notice a sameness to the malt bills, to the color ratings, and, in fact, to other aspects of the recipes. This is simply because this is essentially a book about a single beer style that has been augmented by other ingredients and treatments. Take away those ingredients and treatments and you've got a somewhat narrow interpretation of the IPA style.

Hops

Hops, of course, are the star of the IPA show, whatever else is going on in the beer. The endlessly astonishing array of hop varieties coming out of the Yakima Valley, New Zealand, and various other places is what got us into this whole wonderful mess after all. Despite the narrative of this book focusing on incorporating new and unusual ingredients into recipes and procedures, it is good old hops that make these beers continue to taste like IPA. You will notice a lot of variation from recipe to recipe where hops are concerned.

Only a few of the recipes are very specific about dry hopping. Rather than incorporate repetitive directions as to technique, I offer a general exhortation to add an ounce or two of something from the individual recipe as fermentation concludes, with the option of the same amount added the following day, before removing the beer from the yeast and chilling.

Yeast

Most professional brewers settle on a single yeast strain for most of their beers, perhaps employing a handful of other stalwarts for disparate styles. Within the constraints of a limited number of brewing vessels and a tight production schedule, it isn't practicable for a professional brewery to designate a separate yeast for every beer. This kind of promiscuity is far easier for homebrewers, who are mainly brewing beer for their own consumption and enjoyment, and can, frankly, run circles around their professional counterparts when it comes to closely exploring an array of things, including yeast. Still, it's the pro's job to be aware of what's out there, and to continually defend his or her choices against the endless alternatives.

All that having been said, for the recipes in this book I have chosen a few yeasts with which I am closely familiar. Some of them are familiar to everyone, such as Wyeast's 1056; White Labs WLP002, in my experience, is similar but not identical, and the same can be said for Siebel strain BRY96. The yeast I know best for brewing IPA and other ales is now commercially available through Imperial Organic Yeast in Portland, Oregon as A30 Corporate. The story behind this is that this is the yeast I used while working for one of my former breweries, which has transmogrified into something, well, more corporate than before. A30 Corporate doesn't appear in Imperial's catalog, but commercial brewers can order it by that name. For homebrewers it is offered for sale only a couple of times a year, thus I have included Imperial A07 Flagship in its place for the recipe section. For English-style IPA I love and prefer the yeast that made its clandestine way into this country from the Fuller's brewery in London, the diaspora of which has landed in various labs and in various morphologies. This strain is thermophilic and quirky, but attenuative and can be convinced to be fairly flocculent. A little research will turn it up, should you decide to go that way.

Additional Ingredients

Additional ingredients are listed together and usually include where in the process they are to be introduced. Similar directions are also included in the brewing notes. Late boil additions of solid materials such as herbs, teas, and spices should be bagged in order not to create transfer difficulties, but also to avoid over-extraction by prolonged contact.

3

CRACKING THE CORNUCOPIA

FRUIT AND VEGETABLE IPA

Fruit beers made their appearance fairly early on in the craft movement, but it is only relatively recently that IPAs made with fruit have come into more general production. This has mainly to do with the developing tastes of the audience for whom fruit beers were then and are now intended, as well as an increased tolerance for and recognition of the changes time has wrought on the interpretation of style. Where once the marketing schemes of craft breweries (such as they were in those days) deemed the production of, say, berry, cherry, and apricot beers, employing a lightweight wheat beer base—something intended to appeal to the ladies—these days it is in far more bold and esoteric categories that the use of fruit in brewing has come into its own. Tough guys too, it seems, are willing to drink beers made with fruit. The GABF in 2016 awarded medals to beers brewed with fruit in five separate categories: Fruit Wheat Beer, to be sure; but also Belgian- and American-Style Fruit Beer (IPAs among the latter); Fruited Wood- and Barrel-Aged Sour Beer; and even one in Gluten-Free Beer, which happened to include grapefruit but also happened to be an IPA.

With Belgian fruit *lambic*, such as *framboise* and *kriek*, practically the only historical precedent for beers made with fruit, and also perhaps a cousinly alignment in the brewing world with melomel (mead made with fruit), it was beers using wheat and perhaps honey that provided the earliest conceptual bridge for craft brewers wanting to brew with fruit. The edible-identifiable aspects of wood-aged beers (e.g., coconut, butter, and spices) and the fruity-evocative elements of developing hop varieties have invited into brewing the use of fruit in practically any style, along with vegetables and other fruits of the earth. In many cases, in fact, the burlier and stronger-flavored the beer style, the bolder the additional flavor (or flavors) that can be laid across it—hence the growing popularity and preponderance of fruit-augmented IPA.

BREWING IPA WITH FRUIT

The Taxonomy of Fruit—Who Cares?

In our minds fruits organize themselves into particular culinary types or families. Citrus, for example, includes orange, lemon, grapefruit, tangerine, and lime, but even those relative commoners devolve into more exotic versions: Seville orange, Curaçao orange, blood orange, satsuma, clementine, mandarin, tangelo, Meyer lemon, pomelo, key lime, and kaffir lime; and then there are further varieties such as kumquat, Japanese yuzu, sudachi, and kabosu, and the Jamaican ugli fruit. Citrus fruits are known for their acidity, but vary as to sweetness, ranging from puckeringly tart to downright sugary. Many carry other notes, and have varying levels of bitterness. They can be consumed (or cooked) fresh, whole, peeled, juiced, zested, or any combination thereof. In addition, they can be dried or pickled to add other flavors. There is loads of precedent for the use of citrus in IPA.

Stone fruits are of course another commonly recognized family, including peaches, nectarines, apricots, plums, and cherries. These are also sometimes referred to as soft fruits, since they bruise easily once picked. Again, there are dozens of varieties and hybrids. There are sweet and sour varieties of some of them, such as cherries. Stone fruits are often cooked, despite being easily eaten and worked with raw. IPAs have certainly been brewed with them all, but stone fruits more often find their way into beers of other styles—sour beers, for example, or dark beers such as strong stout. Where other, more tart and bitter fruits may find flavor tie-ins with the resinous terpenes of hops, the generally mellower, earthier, and more openly aromatic stone fruits resonate well with esters generated by fermentation. None of this, however, is absolute: terpenes can be softly fruity and otherwise, esters not always pleasant and mild.

Other tree fruits, such as apples and pears, seem less appropriate for use in brewing IPA; their association with cider and perry is inescapable, as well as possessing aromas that suggest the possible occurrence of acetaldehyde. But, as our aim here is to trample boundaries rather than respect them, I'm going to leave that decision up to you. Especially when one becomes aware of tree fruits like rose hips, crabapples, persimmons, paw paw, and quince, as well as the harder and more tart pears such as Seckel, Bosc, or Dijon. Rose hips? you ask. Roses, in fact, can be grafted onto apple or pear trees, and so bear enough morphological sameness for us to consider them tree fruits. Besides, where else would we put them?

Such debate, if you want to call it that, points out how little we really need to care about classifications for ingredients we're considering using in the brewing of eclectic IPAs. For beyond the abstract satisfaction of conception and paucity of precedent, what we're really after is delicious beer. Is a kumquat a berry, for example? Some would say yes, and be able to back it up. Does that mean it's interchangeable with other fruits more ordinarily identifiable as such? Of course not. So while we're generally interested in fruit groups, it's mainly for the sake of not forgetting anything and being able to reduce the referential chaos somewhat. Paw paw and persimmon, for example, don't quite fit where I put them either, but they do at least grow on trees. But back to it.

Berries too arise in myriad types. We're most familiar with strawberries, blueberries, raspberries, blackberries, and their hybridized ilk (e.g., boysen-berries and marionberries). There are also elderberries, gooseberries, and kiwi fruit. It's tempting to generalize and suggest that these are generally watery, perfumy, and somewhat ephemeral where combining them with hops is concerned, but then there's the tart boldness of gooseberries, themselves invoked when describing New Zealand hop varieties such as Nelson Sauvin.

Speaking of wateriness, perfume, and ephemerality, let's briefly consider the melons, the quiet flavors and aromas of which would likely be swallowed up and overshadowed by aggressive hopping. There are tart and bitter melons (and the horned melon is really more of a cucumber), but I think I speak for many of us when I suggest cantaloupe, honeydew, Persian melon, watermelon, and most others are unlikely to become a trend in regard to being combined with IPA. Still, stranger things have happened.

When taking the varied realm of the tropical fruits into account, it's a good thing we've decided to mainly dispense with taxonomy. For a pineapple is not a mango, nor even remotely a coconut; yet any of these can be evocatively tied to specific and identifiable elements in hop varieties. Lychee, papaya, mangosteen, durian, guava, passion fruit, and on to further realms of tartness in star fruit and Buddha's hand. These are all possibilities IPA-wise. And whether technically tropical or not, cactus fruits such as prickly pear and dragon fruit can additionally, when appropriately colored themselves, add a whole other chromatic dimension to IPAs.

Most of the fruits mentioned previously are either generally common or at least to be found in the specialty produce department at perhaps an Asian or other ethnic specialty market in the United States. Some of them I first encountered on trips to Southeast Asia and Mexico, and followed their progress as they later made their way to the States, often with some kind of fervent and virtuous antioxidant association. Many, once demand was established, have come to be cultivated in the milder North American subclimates; others continue, expensively, to be imported from Asia, Australia, or Central America, arriving individually wrapped in paper or plastic mesh. Stateside, those of us living in areas with large ethnic or immigrant populations have probably had the jump on the rest of you, but even so, crates of once-exotic fruits and products containing such things as mangosteen and açai can these days be found stacked chest high at such prosaic outlets as Costco. With all its conspiracies of shipping and seasonal manipulation, justified by the ever-roving conceit of consumer demand, the world has certainly come to be a smaller place.

Really, Really Exotic Fruits

Anyone who has followed the developing brewing cultures in South America over the past several years is at least vaguely aware of the wonderful, astonishing array of indigenous fruits making their way out of the Amazonian jungle and into beer, particularly in Brazil. In the spring of 2017, it was my good fortune to judge for the first time at the Concurso Brasileiro de Cervejas in Blumenau, Brazil. Included in my duties was the judging of a single round of a category called Brazilian Beer with Fruit. Needless to say, nearly all of the fruits employed in the dozen or so beers we tried were unfamiliar to the non-Brazilian judges at my table. Even the Brazilian judges whose help we enlisted were not entirely familiar with them all; still, they knew more than we did, and usually could at least describe a fruit's appearance and attributes. Fortunately, a sheet outlining and describing some of these fruits was provided. Some carried alternate names with cognate (if obscure) use in English-speaking markets: *graviola*, which we call soursop; *caju*, which, if you think about it, is almost recognizable as cashew, but refers to the larger red or yellow fruit that grows appended to the nut with which we are familiar, and had found its way into a delicious, kettle-soured Berliner *weiss*-type beer; and then there's *cupuaçu*, the Latin name for which (*Theobroma grandiflorum*) at least recalls Dogfish Head's chili-chocolate beer of several years back, Theobroma. But beyond that we are generally at sea, at least without a bilingual fruit taxonomist in tow. There's *cagaita, jabuticaba, jatoba, baru* (also known as *cumaru*), and *cajá*, which is also called *tapaebà* (also not to be confused with the aforementioned caju). And that was just one round—there were dozens of other entries.

BREWING IPA WITH VEGETABLES

Is telling someone to brew with vegetables the same as urging them to eat vegetables? For in the realm of the earth's regenerative bounty it has to be admitted that, even for vegetarians (I'm guessing), vegetables are somewhat less exciting than fruits. Vegetable aromas are, well, vegetabley, less ethereal and sweet than fruit aromas; vegetable flavors are heartier and prosaically better-seeming for you; and the essence of vegetables is more nutritive than immediately gratifying. Vegetables are something you know you ought to consume; fruits, with their seasonal ripening, and the baking and jam-making, and whatever else you do to prolong the time you spend with them and the benefit you gain from them, are something you really, truly enjoy.

In the Land of the Mangaboos

Lest this section seem an apologia for vegetables, there are wonderful and tasty things to be done with them in the crafting of interesting and ground-breaking IPAs. It's true that vegetables don't put themselves forward in the obvious way that fruits do in combination with hop essences and residual esters, but there are a lot of vegetables that carry spicy notes, palate effects, complex sweetness (often more so when cooked), and various elements that can combine well with other ingredients, such as herbs, spices, or fruits, the latter especially so if they are, somehow, conceptually or taxonomically related.

But once again, let's deal with classification. Nerdy children (like I was) amuse themselves with the sphinxian question of whether a tomato is a fruit or a vegetable. Others wonder about melons and gourds, including cucumber and pumpkin. A college friend of mine was allergic to anything that grew with seeds on the inside; that, perhaps, is the most authoritative and personalized method of binary differentiation. Still, we don't care.

There are, first of all, some things that will never work in beer, never mind the specialized requirements of IPA. Anything remotely cabbagey, for starters. Cabbage, when properly pickled, cooked, or otherwise dressed up, can be delicious, economical, and nutritious. But there's no mistaking cabbage's sulfury stank, er, effect that takes it out of the running for inclusion in a beverage intended for refreshment. Some yeasts generate sulfur, and we do all we can to let them get it out of their systems by aging; the last thing we want is to put sulfurous compounds back into beer. And this isn't just cabbage, as you probably know. It's broccoli, it's cauliflower, it's a lot of leafy greens, including their roots such as radishes, turnips, and rutabagas. Onions as well are generally taboo in pretty much all forms. Given that some hop descriptors include references to onion or garlic in a pejorative sense, it's worth pointing out that intense cognate flavors when augmenting IPAs can sometimes heighten imbalance rather than mitigate it. Although, it must be said, when putting together a recipe of any kind for drinkers to enjoy, flavors present themselves in natural combinations which themselves are entirely subjective. By the way, never mind about the tomato—I doubt we'll be using that to make IPA either.

But wait, what about beets and parsnips? What about carrots? Those somehow seem more plausible, but their consideration reinforces the case-by-case nature of all of this. One thing those have is sugar, I'm guessing in greater abundance than many other vegetables. They also have, in some cases such as carrots and parsnips, a spicy kind of brightness, or essence, that makes one think more of uplifting lightness than lumpen heaviness.

It's a far different thing, we all know—or at least those of us engaged and conscientious enough to have visited our friends the hop farmers in their native habitat—to pull apart a green hop cone in the field and smell its just-off-the-bine essence than to taste that same hop in the beer. Rubbing kilned and finished whole hops is an intermediate experience, once again only partly indicative of an eventual beer. Still, it's the way we evaluate things, extrapolating by our experience and intuition to figure out what we will be able to accomplish.

Similarly, in order to get a feel for what any vegetable (or fruit, for that matter) will bring to a beer, and how well it will combine with other elements of that beer, one sometimes needs to appreciate different stages of its life cycle. Nuance emerges, we all know, with decomposition; fermentation itself is a kind of controlled spoilage, or at least a biochemical reduction. And it's sometimes necessary to experience, or at least imagine, the flavors and aromas that can arise as materials are transformed, whether it's pleasantly through cooking, perhaps, or less so by way of degrading to its simpler elements.

For those of us who like them, fresh young peas are one of the crowning joys of summer, but if you've driven through pea fields on warm nights during harvest time, or better yet been on hand as pea silage is taken from storage on its way to feeding cattle, you probably won't want to put peas in your beer. Peas also, in their general leguminous funk, wouldn't lend themselves effectively to the kinds of bold and sharply-flavored beers we're talking about here. Corn, though wonderfully sweet and flavorful when fresh, also carries shades of dimethyl sulfide (DMS), an unpleasant association for brewers and seen as indicative of an inexpertly managed boil or fermentation. The last thing we want is for things we've purposely added as flavor enhancements to register on the palates of our critics and customers as false markers of flawed procedure.

And yet, as my favorite fruit writer David Karp has observed, sometimes the tastiest fruit is what you pick up off the ground. Sometimes nice things appear in these phases of transition, and I mainly mean in the judicious cooking of fruits and vegetables. As a brewer I'm forced to admit a greater tolerance for stuff in my refrigerator beginning to "go bad" than some of those I've lived with. Brewers are able to imagine the Maillard reactions that occur as sugars react with amino acids, pleasantly conjuring up the development of complex flavors. Outside of the malthouse or brewery this is what happens in general when we cook things, particularly things of lesser acidity. For vegetables that show an almost generic fresh aroma when first cut in their raw state, imagining these changes is the best way to understand how we might use them. Carrots are a bit this way, and peppers certainly are, particularly the sweeter, non-green ones. (Onions display a lot of caramel sweetness when browned, but I think we've already pretty much laid their contribution to our discussion to rest.) In any case, to judge the appropriateness of some of these potential ingredients, we sometimes need to cook or roast them. Not just peppers, but pumpkins and squash give up their main flavorful essence through roasting; they are otherwise watery and astringent. Does any of this remind you of the earlier, possibly overly dismissive, mention of the perfume and wateriness of some melons, berries, and other fruits? Good.

Well, we've come to peppers, haven't we? And since we have, it's time to pre-emptively lay to rest the notion that chilies are a spice rather than a vegetable or fruit. If, like cinnamon, the spicy element of chilies was harvested by peeling the outer layer of their stems (or something), or if perhaps their seeds were the only place in which capsaicin resided, then we might, like the seeds of celery or cilantro, be justified in teasing these constituent parts away from the greater organism. But on this taxonomic issue anyway there's no reason to stray. One interpretive effect of the Brazilian fruit cupuaçu is of a eucalyptus-like anesthetic tingle (ditto Szechuan pepper, in a way). Does that, like capsicum, cry out to be its own thing? I don't think so. Once again, as far as our use of them in IPA goes, applications of which are rampant, where chilies are classified doesn't really matter.

I Must Have Fruit!

Recently I was part of a sort of brewers' retreat, where a group of several professional brewers, lots of maniacal homebrewers, beer enthusiasts, and game spouses convened at Devil's Thumb resort in Colorado to brew with more established pros on pre-devised themes. I was one of the latter, and when posed with the question of what I would set out to brew with these folks it struck me (obviously) to do something along the lines of this book. First I put together a basic malt bill of 74% Rahr® Pale Ale, 10% Rahr White Wheat, 8% Weyermann® Munich, and 4% each of Weyermann Carahell® and Crisp 45°L crystal. Then I requested an array of hops distinctive and fruity/herbal enough to combine with whatever additional ingredients the group decided to use from the selection I brought along. Among the hops chosen were a couple of stalwart American fruity varieties (Citra and Mosaic), a couple of fruitier-yet New Zealand types (Nelson Sauvin and Dr. Rudi), an Australian variety (Galaxy) for good measure, and two German varieties with somewhat different conceptual purposes (Hallertau Blanc for a different kind of fruitiness, and Northern Brewer in case we might need a complementary hop should the group choose a resinous or particularly terpenic herb).

I had a lot of ideas, of course, but I knew I'd have to go with what I could get, so I called my friend Alex Leedy, with whom in her role as ingredient procurer for New Belgium for a number of years I had had fairly close contact. (Alex now has her own company to supply small-scale pros and homebrewers with fruit juices, purees, and concentrates.) We talked about what might appeal and make sense for the assignment, given her stores and the sizes appropriate to the scale of the task. So, when I arrived in the mountains I had a cooler chock-full of fruits citrus and tropical: guava, pineapple, tangerine, lulo, tamarind, blood orange, calamansi, and the Japanese triumvirate of yuzu, sudachi, and kabosu, along with a couple of outliers such as aronia berries (an intense and somewhat seedy berry of the northern plains, also known as chokeberry and, according to a Canadian in the group, similar to Saskatoon berry). In the meantime, I hit up a number of more prosaic sources of my own: a couple of co-ops in Seattle and San Francisco, a Whole Foods in Colorado, a Japanese market, and my neighbor's rosemary bush. From all these sources I gathered (in addition to the neighbor's rosemary) thyme, kaffir lime leaves, shiso, chilies, juniper berries, cardamom pods, and a box of tea made up of turmeric, ginger, and Meyer lemon that looked interesting. Just for good measure, and in case somebody wanted something to do in the late stages of the boil, I threw in a couple of bags of lemons and a Microplane® zester, an essential piece of equipment for this and other kitchen and brewery jobs.

The first item of business was deciding what we were going to brew, so while our compatriots got in line to mill their grains and get the jump on us, we passed around jugs, vials, tubs, leaves, and bags of this and that, tasting and rubbing and bruising, closing our eyes and imagining what things might taste like together and in some combination with the hops we had secondarily to choose from. A few fruity suggestions seemed to prevail, so we put together an imprecise blend of things in a cup that we passed around, subject to adjustment and proportion. What we struck on was a blend of pineapple puree and tamarind concentrate, enlivened by a dash of sudachi juice, which is a Japanese citrus variety that carries a slight effect of black pepper. We also decided to add a couple of chopped habaneros (for an approximately 10-gallon batch) with a secondary addition of sudachi juice at the time of the prospective second dry hopping. When the time came, we sat down and figured out the hops, shooting for about 65 IBU:

2.0 oz. (56 g) Citra (13.2% AA) @ 60 min.

1.0 oz. (28 g) Citra (13.2% AA) @ 30 min.

2.0 oz. (56 g) Hallertau Blanc (8.8% AA) @ 30 min.

1.25 oz. (35 g) Dr. Rudi (13.2% AA) @ 2 min.

1.25 oz. (35 g) Galaxy (15.2% AA) @ 2 min.

1.25 oz. (35 g) Dr. Rudi (13.2% AA) @ whirlpool

1.25 oz. (35 g) Galaxy (15.2% AA) @ whirlpool

1.25 oz. approx. (35 g approx.) each of Galaxy and Dr. Rudi on two successive days of dry-hopping: one when fermentation was nearly complete, and the other the following day, this time along with the chopped habaneros in sudachi juice as well.

All fruits were added in the fermentor at the same time we pitched basic Chico yeast.

A second group the next day chose a different blend of things: guava, shiso, and kabosu (another Japanese citrus that suggests melon), this time in much greater proportion than we had added sudachi the previous day. Hopping for this beer followed a similar pattern to the first day, but we substituted Nelson Sauvin for Galaxy, used Dr. Rudi instead of Citra for bittering, and also moved Hallertau Blanc into the late and dry hop additions.

It was a tropical party for sure (aside from the snow falling outside as we brewed) and among these folks there was a distinct preference for fruit over other, quieter ingredients. While I encourage this kind of flourish and experimentation, there's a lot to be said for greater subtlety and less aggressive interplay through the use of herbs and spices, vegetables, and teas—touches that in some cases people may not even be able to name (or markedly notice), but which can make for a pretty interesting and conceptually nuanced IPA.

BROTHER, CAN YOU SPARE A SOURCE?

Putting Your Hands on All This Stuff

Of course, small-scale brewing lends itself more readily to any kind of experimentation involving the use of new or unusual ingredients. Where a homebrewer making five gallons of beer at a time can achieve an effect with the addition of a literal handful of this or that, even a medium-sized pro is either mobilizing his or her kitchen staff (if they have one) for the day to roast, poach, peel, stem, juice, or puree, or they are sourcing things that arrive shipped in buckets, boxes, or mylar bags. Bigger brewers, of course, think in totes, drums, even tankers, especially as successful experimentation is dubiously rewarded with the kind of demand that makes the ongoing production of new and interesting beers a logistical challenge. All this assuming the quantities necessary to keep on keepin' on are even available, especially once that other brewery across town (or across the country) gets wind of what a great response you're getting to your neat and idiosyncratic idea. Remember when blood orange beers were new? But we didn't really used to have to actively source hops either (nor, to add a mitigating note, were we really able to the extent we are today).

Well once more the world has changed. And yet, it's still about relationships. While address books, even the Rolodex®, has gone the way of the pteranodon, not to have some kind of comprehensive list of contacts for the sourcing of specialty ingredients is to pretty much take one's self out of the game where the crafting of new and innovative beers is concerned. The upside is that these days there are people out there, and the specialty companies they work for, ready to do their best to get you what you need in whatever form you need it. And once you make their list as somebody habitually enquiring about the new and unusual, they're also likely to tip you off once something interesting creeps into the market. Larger craft breweries have people, even sometimes whole departments, dedicated to the acquisition of specialty ingredients, often writing contracts to ensure ongoing availability and specific source parameters.

The brewers at such pioneering stalwarts as Anchor and Sierra Nevada didn't spend a minute during their early days sourcing such esoterica, but I assure you they do today. Good luck with all that Brazilian stuff, by the way.

Grow Your Own to Brew Your Own

Before we go any further, let's consider for a moment how indescribably cool it is to grow your own specialty ingredients yourself, and your own fruits in particular. As big an investment as farmland (or even a garden) can be—and I hasten to observe that this is not a book about agriculture—if you have the land and the inclination, growing produce yourself is a fabulous way to assure the supply of something for yourself, possibly at less expense (and it's a great story to tell); this is especially the case if others are scratching their heads about how to get their hands on any at all, at any price.

Foraging, too, is a big endeavor these days, though a word of caution: make absolutely certain you're gathering what you think you are, and that it's non-toxic and officially cleared for use in beers later being offered for sale. People occasionally inadvertently kill themselves with misidentified mushrooms, for example. Possibilities abound in the natural world for toxic effect, even among representatives of a single species or, more specifically, from one part of a plant to another—tasty and harmless leaves needing to be separated from toxic and dangerous stems, say (or vice versa). For example, the manioc for beers made in South American jungles needs to be boiled to eliminate toxicity; sometimes drying, separating, cooking, or otherwise processing ingredients is necessary to make them palatable at the very least. If you're a homebrewer you're less bound by all this from a liability point of view, but in the interest of safety would it inconvenience you so much to look at a field guide, or poke around a bit online, before you actually do anything with that proverbial handful you've gathered?

Form Follows Function (or Is It the Other Way Around?)

Herbs and spices figure prominently in our quest, but fruit is probably the pre-eminent specialty ingredient in the market for making augmented, or eclectic, beers in general and, for our purposes, IPAs in particular. And in this light, it is necessary to review the different forms of fruit matter, the different products and treatments available from various sources, as well as the ways in which each of them is to be introduced, the things to watch out for, and the relative effects that each brings to the table of innovation and tastiness.

Whole fruit is the simplest and most comprehensible way to go when augmenting your beer, whether you pick it yourself, buy it at the market, order it from individual orchards or farms, or source it from larger, more combinative fruit suppliers. For now, never mind the fact that most fruits are comprised of different, and differently flavored, parts; we'll get into more of that later. And when I say "whole" I mean all of it, but not necessarily in one discrete piece. It isn't cheating, as far as I'm concerned, to have whole fruit you've ordered from a supplier arrive crushed, pureed, frozen, sterilized, or whatever. As with so many things we do, one is continually free to choose which elements of the process one feels the need to, literally, put one's hand to.

To put things in perspective when considering the use of concentrates or extracts, whole fruit, even if processed, is considered single strength. The ratings that appear on whatever spec sheet accompanies it expresses a fruit's sugar concentration (typically in degrees Brix) as they might have been taken with a refractometer from a single typical fruit in the batch. Concentrates are produced in various degrees, but the thing to pay attention to is that sugar rating. This is the amount of sweetness (and fermentable sugar) the batch of fruit will contribute to your recipe relative to the volume of material. It's to be hoped that flavor and aroma and perhaps color will survive the rigors of fermentation (otherwise why bother?), but sugar concentration is the number to plug in when projecting contributions to extract and eventual alcoholic content. Purists among us might consider the use of concentrates somewhat less than honest, and that may also apply to the ways in which concentrates are often handled, with pumps and lifts and in-line dosing systems, but when an operation is of a certain size, the person-hour alternative makes the expense, and the ease, of taking the path of concentrates acceptable. All in the interest of delicious beer, right?

Whole fruits are also available powdered and freeze-dried, and it will be a matter of availability and experience when deciding which is appropriate for use; you may decide they taste better, or that in the quantities you are required to order the powdered or freeze-dried option holds better than partial bags or buckets of otherwise processed fruit products. No judgement here, once again.

It is with some ambivalence that I include the notion of using manufactured fruit flavors and essences for augmenting your IPA (or any other craft-produced fruit beer). You'll notice I didn't use the word artificial. It has become vitally important for the multi-billion dollar companies that produce such flavors for use in mass-produced sodas, snack foods, and many other products (which literally fill supermarkets outside of the fresh produce aisles), to engineer combinations of naturally occurring compounds in a kind of Frankensteiny way that allows them to (arguably) legitimately call the final product natural. Using the F-word in that last sentence may have been gratuitous, but, to my mind, lemon oil extracted from lemon myrtle isn't actually lemon, nor, in all likelihood, does that strawberry-kiwi energy drink you recently drank contain much, if any, actual strawberry or kiwi. In recent years kits from some of these manufacturers of fruit flavors and essences have circulated among brewers, offering the shortcut of a vial to create the effect of melon, guava, peach, or pine. The ones I've sniffed haven't been particularly right-on, but even if they were perfect, to me they still wouldn't smell quite right. Still, we all must do what our hearts tell us, including what we can afford or are willing to put up with. All this coming from a man who once used Yellow #6 to dye a pumpkin malt liquor orange—it was ironic, what can I say?

The Morality of It All

I once made a beer using 75 or so pounds of the biggest, plumpest, most perfectly ripe Rainier cherries I'd ever seen. Partly for social media effect, but also because I hadn't figured out a better way to do it, I crushed them with my feet, stepping up and down in a 35-gallon plastic drum. As I was doing so, I wondered if maybe there wasn't something a little bit wrong about converting top-grade comestible material into a negligible flavor effect in a nominal quantity (10 barrels) of beer. And I have to say, I don't have an answer for that. I've always considered toiletry products such as shampoo and lotion made with avocados, key lime, and such as a touch profligate. Aloe vera at least has a soothing, anesthetic effect; but you can make pulque out of it too.

Is it wrong, in this age of inequitable possession and disproportionate satiety, to divert our food supply to make beer? One could argue both ways: there's the puritanical view that making beer out of barley malt undermines otherwise edible inventory; and there's the epicurean's take that it's right if it makes it delicious. I have to say that I am most fulfilled when able to use fruit that my produce guy can't unload elsewhere and might otherwise simply rot to nothing, but I also haven't lost sleep when I've used something delectable—like those Rainier cherries, like some wonderful Skagit Valley gooseberries I had similar qualms about—in the pursuit of my brewing life's aim of making something that will please my friends and customers.

It would probably bother me to make a fruit or vegetable beer on such a scale that it deprives the hungry of sustenance and the desirous of enjoyment, but I have in the past contracted for many tens of thousands of pounds of pumpkin, and once owned and brewed with all the elderflowers at that moment available for sale in North America. I'm the first person I know who brewed with yuzu, a one-time rare Japanese delicacy, a few drops of which make the matsutake sing. Pumpkin, it must be said, is a Morlock of the vegetable world (or is it fruit?); elderflower is not really edible at all, and if we can keep some of it out of the hands of those St. Germain folks, all the better. But the question is still something to consider when contemplating the use of things that could be put to better, more fruitful use.

EXPERIENCING (AND ANALYZING) THE FLAVOR ELEMENTS

The Sensuous Brewer

Consider the experience of eating a fruit. Depending on what it is, you may have needed to peel it first; whether with a knife or with your hands, even that process is a part of experiencing what that fruit is. If it's a citrus fruit, you no doubt triggered an explosion of volatile oils as you plunged your thumb beneath the surface of the skin, and smelled and felt the pulpy white stuff between the actual outside and what we consider the essence of the fruit. If it's an apple or a pear, by the time you've removed the peel (let's hope all in one piece) you're already experiencing the alteration of aroma due to oxidation; it's simply duller and flavorfully different than that bright initial appley aroma. If it's a peach or an apricot that you've simply bitten into, aside from the fuzz, you've also experienced the tannic resistance of the peel, the slipperiness and overwhelming juicy sweetness of the flesh, and eventually the quandary of the pit.

We could go on in this vein for a while, but the point has been made that there are many elements to identify and evaluate when considering the experience of a fruit and to what degree it is appropriate to build them into an IPA. That oil in the citrus peel? A resounding yes to combining it with the essential oils inherent in the hops you've decided to use. Even the astringency of the pith can be combined with the bitterness of the beer to add complexity. The juice (though probably not the membranous material separating the sections), that's your flavor essence, with all it brings through acidity and sweetness. The fast-fading brightness of apples and pears may not be as appropriate for the kind of beers we're talking about, but who knows? And those peaches and apricots, depending on the variety and degree of ripeness, may be just the thing, like the citrus fruit but in a whole different way, tying in the esters produced by fermentation. We still need to figure out what to do with those pits . . .

Different fruits lend themselves to being used in different ways. The peel of the grapefruit or lime, for example, is more easily separated from the rest of the fruit than is that of the cherry or apricot; the oils inherent in the citrus peel also provide distinctive aromas. These different constituents should be introduced at the appropriate time. The juice of those grapefruits or limes, for example, will probably show itself best if introduced either at fermentation or later, while the zested peel could give a nice aromatic effect when tossed into the whirlpool or used as a "dry zest" addition a day or two prior to crashing temperature. Also, think twice about simply discarding any peels or seeds; if nothing else they could perhaps go into the mash. It's not only a sound concept, it pays homage to a sort of stem-to-snout ethos.

Some things, however, are more appropriate than others. The crushed or juiced seeds of the pomegranate are the show, of course, and even the pits of cherries and other soft fruits can impart an almond note (also perhaps a bit of cyanide—be warned); the uncrushed seeds of citrus or apples, on the other hand, will likely contribute nothing and possibly cause mechanical problems down the line. And yet you aren't liable to find any use for those fast-oxidizing kiwi peels or melon rinds other than shredding them and adding them to the mash. As an aside, masticating juicers separate peels out and deposit them in their little hopper; if you're brewing on the kind of scale where the use of such a device is appropriate, and my own 20-barrel brewery found them useful (though turn them off and let the motor rest from time to time), what's the harm in tossing all that material into the mash?

What It Is We're Trying to Do Here

The main thing to remember in all of this is that, in general, the earlier things are added to the brewing process, the more nuanced the effect will be on the finished beer. Where fruits are concerned, little can be gained by a mash addition, aside from those peels, say, providing a little utilitarian help with fermentable sugar or possibly oblique flavor. Adding lovely ripe fruit at this stage is simply a waste. Sure, you'll get some fermentable material, but your yeast either won't recognize the fructose or glucose molecules you've provided in this way as being any different from simple sugars arising from your all-malt mash, or it may in fact favor the fructose and glucose over good old maltose, which could protract the lag time before fermentation of malt sugars commences. Something resinous and tenacious is a different story when we consider flavors that endure through the wort, like juniper, for example.

Additions to fermentation must be similarly considered; fruit sugars are simple enough to be fermented on their own (but may, as mentioned above, protract the lag time) and residual flavor will likely remain in some measure.

Still, adding whole or processed fruit even now won't yield the bang for your buck that cramming it in through the bung of that barrel or pasteurizing it and adding it in-line on the way to packaging will (though these methods can present stability issues with the beer itself). This is not the same thing, I hasten to say, as suggesting that you shouldn't do it; adding fruit in fermentation is in fact the most common way to make fruit beers. There's also something to be said for subtlety; to get the greatest fruity effect is not necessarily the aim of the brewer when making nuanced and balanced beers. In short, you'll get the greatest theoretical contribution of all if you add things at every stage, but that can be expensive and exhausting.

Consider the use of fruit in producing endlessly varied and interesting IPAs a kind of template for much of what will be covered in the rest of this book. That said, there's so much variety in the world of fruit and so many ways in which its various types, forms, parts, and aspects can be employed, that it's almost impossible to cover it all in narrative form. As we move on to other realms of eclecticism, I refer you to the charts at the end of this chapter (tables 3.1 and 3.2), which outline the myriad uses fruits and vegetables can be put to as you are crafting an IPA the world has heretofore never seen or appreciated.

The following recipes—and for that matter all the recipes in this book—are intended to display the use of different types of ingredients introduced in different ways, in the most subjective way possible. Your taste or the expectations of your friends and customers will no doubt dictate alterations in proportion, as well as specific substitutions based on availability, season, miraculous discovery, or some idea you've developed on your own.

IPA RECIPES WITH FRUIT

Cranberries for Sal IPA *(For 5 US gallons [19 L])*

Cranberry New England IPA

Original gravity: 1.070 (7.5°P) (without fruit)
Final gravity: 1.015 (3.75°P)
Color: 4.95 SRM (without fruit)
Bitterness: 58 IBU
ABV: 7% (with fruit)

GRAIN BILL
70% 12 lb. (5.5 kg) artisanally malted pale malt (local if you can get it)
12% 2 lb. (1 kg) malted wheat
9% 1.5 lb. (0.75 kg) flaked barley
9% 1.5 lb. (0.75 kg) flaked oats

HOPS
2.5 oz. (70g) Chinook (13% AA) @ 90 min.
1.0 oz. (28 g) Cascade (5.5% AA) @ 10 min.
1.5 oz. (42 g) Cascade (5.5% AA) @ 2 min.
1.0 oz. (28 g) Cascade (5.5% AA) @ whirlpool

ADDITIONAL INGREDIENTS
1.0 oz. (28 g) orange zest (variety optional—consider Seville or Curaçao)
    @ whirlpool
3 lb. (1.36 kg) cranberry puree

YEAST
Imperial Yeast A07 Flagship

BREWING NOTES
Mash 60 min. @ 153°F (67°C).
Boil 90 min.
Add orange zest to whirlpool.
Dilute cranberry puree in enough wort to liquefy, and recombine.
Ferment until terminal, then transfer to secondary.
Condition @ 35°F (2°C) for 1 week until bright.
Carbonate to 2.5 volumes (4.9 g/L) CO_2.

Hot Guava Monster IPA *(For 5 US gallons [19 L])*

Guava Habanero Double IPA

Original gravity: 1.080 (20°P)
Final gravity: 1.017 (4.25°P)
Color: 5.28 SRM (without fruit)
Bitterness: 75 IBU
ABV: 8.5%

GRAIN BILL
82.5% 13 lb. (5.9 kg) Great Western Malting Northwest Select 2-row malt
13% 2 lb. (910 g) Great Western Malting White Wheat malt
3% 8 oz. (225 g) Weyermann Munich malt
1.5% 4 oz. (112 g) Weyermann Carahell malt

HOPS
2.3 oz. (65 g) Magnum (12% AA) @ 90 min.
1.5 oz. (42 g) Motueka (7% AA) @ 10 min.
1.5 oz. (42 g) Mosaic (12.25% AA) @ 2 min.
1.0 oz. (28 g) Motueka (7% AA) @ whirlpool
1.5 oz. (42 g) Motueka (7% AA) @ dry hop 1st day (when almost terminal)
1.5 oz. (42 g) Mosaic (12.25% AA) @ dry hop 1st day (when almost terminal)
1.0 oz. (28 g) Motueka (7% AA) @ dry hop 2nd day
1.0 oz. (28 g) Mosaic (12.25% AA) @ dry hop 2nd day

ADDITIONAL INGREDIENTS
7 lb. (3.2 kg) guava puree
2–3 chopped habaneros (with or without seeds)

YEAST
Wyeast 1056

BREWING NOTES
Mash 60 min. @ 153°F (67°C).
Boil 90 min.
Dilute guava puree in wort and reintroduce at pitching.
Ferment until terminal, then transfer to secondary.
Chop habaneros and introduce to secondary/conditioning.
Condition @ 35°F (2°C) 1 week until bright.
Carbonate to 2.5 volumes (4.9 g/L) CO_2.

Fuyu Me IPA *(For 5 US gallons [19 L])*

Persimmon Long Pepper IPA

Original gravity: 1.068 (17°P)
Final gravity: 1.019 (4.75°P)
Color: 7.58 SRM (without fruit)
Bitterness: 60 IBU
ABV: 6.4%

GRAIN BILL
90% 11 lb. (5 kg) American 2-row malt
4% 8 oz. (225 g) Weyermann Munich malt
3% 6 oz. (170 g) Weyermann Carared® malt
3% 6 oz. (170 g) Crisp 70°L crystal malt

HOPS

3.25 oz. (92 g) Glacier (5.6% AA) @ 90 min.
1.5 oz. (42 g) Hallertauer Blanc (5.6% AA) @ 5 min.
1.5 oz. (42 g) Rakau (10.5% AA) @ 5 min.
0.5 oz. (14 g) Hallertauer Blanc (5.6% AA) @ 2 min.
0.5 oz. (14 g) Rakau (10.5% AA) @ 2 min.
1.0 oz. (28 g) Hallertauer Blanc (5.6% AA) @ whirlpool
1.0 oz. (28 g) Rakau (10.5% AA) @ whirlpool

ADDITIONAL INGREDIENTS

2 lb. (910 g) Fuyu persimmons, cored and pureed (**note:** do not use Hachiya
     persimmons unless ripe and sweet—taste and you will definitely know)
1.0 oz. (28 g) Sumatran long pepper

YEAST

Imperial Yeast A07 Flagship

BREWING NOTES

Mash 60 min. @ 153°F (67°C).
Boil 90 min.
Dilute persimmon puree with wort and reintroduce.
Ferment with persimmon until terminal, then transfer to secondary.
Condition with long pepper @ 35°F (2°C) 1 week until bright.
Carbonate to 2.5 volumes (4.9 g/L) CO_2.

ADDITIONAL NOTES

Persimmons are ripe when the core attached to the stem and leaves separates
readily from the fruit. Anyone who has ever tasted unripe persimmon will
never forget the mouth-drying experience.

Punch Drunk Love DIPA *(For 5 US gallons [19 L])*

Fruit Punchy Double IPA

Thanks to Steve Luke of Cloudburst Brewing Co., Seattle, Washington.

Original gravity: 1.072 (18°P)
Final gravity: 1.010 (2.5°P)
Color: 6.2 SRM (without fruit)
Bitterness: 60 IBU
ABV: 6.8%

GRAIN BILL
96.5% 14 lb. (6.4 kg) Rahr 2-row malt
2% 5 oz. (140 g) Thomas Fawcett Pale Crystal malt
1% 2.5 oz. (70 g) Weyermann Carared malt
0.5% 1.0 oz. (28 g) Weyermann Special W® malt

HOPS
0.5 oz (14 g) Sorachi Ace (13% AA) @ 90 min.
0.25 oz. (7 g) Cascade (5.5% AA) @ 15 min.
0.25 oz. (7 g) Citra (12% AA) @ 5 min.
0.25 oz. (7 g) Cascade (5.5% AA) @ 5 min.
0.25 oz. (7 g) "HBC 344" (10.5% AA) @ 5 min.
1.0 oz. (28 g) Citra (12% AA) @ whirlpool
1.0 oz. (28 g) Mosaic (12.25% AA) @ whirlpool
1.0 oz. (28 g) "HBC 344" (10.5% AA) @ whirlpool
1.5 oz. (42 g) Citra (12% AA) @ dry hop
1.5 oz. (42 g) Mosaic (12.25% AA) @ dry hop
1.5 oz. (42 g) "HBC 344" (10.5% AA) @ dry hop

ADDITIONAL INGREDIENTS
1.6 lb. (725 g) sweet cherry puree
0.75 lb. (340 g) pineapple puree

YEAST
Imperial Yeast A07 Flagship

BREWING NOTES

Mash 60 min. @ 153°F (67°C).

Boil 90 min.

Dilute fruit purees with wort and reintroduce prior to pitching yeast.

Ferment @ 68°F (20°C) until gravity is 1.016, then bump to 70°F (21°C).

Dry hop warm for 4 days, then crash to 35°F (2°C).

Condition @ 35°F (2°C) 1 week until bright.

Carbonate to 2.5 volumes (4.9 g/L) CO_2.

Yuzulupululu IPA *(For 5 US gallons [19 L])*

Yuzu IPA

Original gravity: 1.066 (16.5°P)
Final gravity: 1.019 (4.75°P)
Color: 3.85 SRM
Bitterness: 55 IBU
ABV: 6.3%

GRAIN BILL

72.5% 8.5 lb. (3.9 kg) German Pilsner malt

21.5% 2.5 lb. (1.2 kg) German wheat malt

4% 8 oz. (225 g) Weyermann Munich malt

2% 4 oz. (112 g) Weyermann Carapils® malt

HOPS

1.5 oz. (42 g) Sorachi Ace (13% AA) @ 90 min.

1.5 oz. (42 g) Amarillo (9.2% AA) @ 10 min.

0.5 oz. (14 g) Amarillo (9.2% AA) @ 2 min.

2 oz. (56 g) Citra (12% AA) @ whirlpool

ADDITIONAL INGREDIENTS

9 fl. oz. (270 mL) yuzu juice

1.5 oz. (42 g) lemon zest (or yuzu zest if using whole fruit)

YEAST

Imperial Yeast A07 Flagship

BREWING NOTES

Mash 60 min. @ 153°F (67°C).

Boil 90 min.

Add lemon zest in whirlpool.

Ferment with 6 fl. oz. (180 mL) yuzu juice until terminal, then transfer to secondary.

Add remaining 3 fl. oz. (90 mL) yuzu juice to secondary.

Condition @ 35°F (2°C) 1 week until bright

Carbonate to 2.5 volumes (4.9 g/L) CO_2.

South Island Hiss IPA *(For 5 US gallons [19 L])*

Gooseberry IPA

Original gravity: 1.069 (17.25°P)
Final gravity: 1.014 (2.5°P)
Color: 4.74 SRM (without fruit)
Bitterness: 68 IBU
ABV: 7.2%

GRAIN BILL

81% 11 lb. (5 kg) palest 2-row malt you can get, preferably micro-malted

15% 2 lb. (910 g) malted wheat

2% 4 oz. (112 g) Weyermann Munich malt

2% 4 oz. (112 g) Weyermann Carahell malt

HOPS

1.5 oz. (42g) CTZ* (15.5% AA) @ 90 min.

1.5 oz. (42 g) Nelson Sauvin (12% AA) @ 10 min.

1.5 oz. (42 g) Nelson Sauvin (12% AA) @ 2 min.

0.5 oz. (14 g) Nelson Sauvin (12% AA) @ whirlpool

*A blend of Columbus, Tomahawk®, and Zeus.

ADDITIONAL INGREDIENTS

8 lb. (3.6 kg) fresh or frozen gooseberries (or use pre-pureed)

YEAST
Imperial Yeast A07 Flagship

BREWING NOTES
Mash 60 min. at 153°F (67°C).
Boil 90 min.
Puree 8 lb. (3.6 kg) fresh or frozen gooseberries (if not using pre-pureed) to dilute with wort and add to fermentation.
Ferment until terminal, then transfer to secondary.
Condition @ 35°F (2°C) 1 week until bright.
Carbonate to 2.5 volumes (4.9 g/L) CO_2.

Red Spruce IPA *(For 5 US gallons [19 L])*

Redcurrant Spruce IPA

Original gravity: 1.065 (16.25°P)
Final gravity: 1.018 (4.5°P)
Color: 7.63 SRM
Bitterness: 64 IBU
ABV: 6.1%

GRAIN BILL
85% 10 lb. (4.54 kg) American 2-row malt
8.5% 1 lb. (454 g) Belgian aromatic malt
4.25% 8 oz. (225 g) Weyermann Munich malt
2.25% 4 oz. (112 g) Weyermann Carahell malt

HOPS
1.25 oz. (35 g) Waimea (17.5% AA) @ 90 min.
1.5 oz. (42 g) Dr. Rudi (11% AA) @ 10 min.
0.5 oz. (14 g) Simcoe (13% AA) @ 2 min.
1.5 oz. (42 g) Dr. Rudi (11% AA) @ whirlpool

ADDITIONAL INGREDIENTS
6 oz. (170 g) redcurrants (crushed or juice)
6 oz. (170 g) spruce tips

YEAST
Wyeast 1056

BREWING NOTES
Mash 60 min. @ 153°F (67°C).
Boil 90 min.
Ferment with redcurrants until terminal, then transfer to secondary.
Add spruce to secondary.
Condition @ 35°F (2°C) 1 week until bright.
Carbonate to 2.5 volumes (4.9 g/L) CO_2.

True North Grapefruit IPA *(For 5 US gallons [19 L])*

Grapefruit IPA

Modified from Ballast Point (original Sculpin) Polaris IPA with a grapefruit addition. Thanks to Colby Chandler of Ballast Point Brewing, San Diego, California for help with this.

Original gravity: 1.054 (13.5°P)
Final gravity: 1.013 (3.1°P)
Color: 4 SRM
Bitterness: 84 IBU
ABV: 5.4%

GRAIN BILL
91% 10 lb. (4.54 kg) Great Western Malting's Northwest Select 2-row malt
9% 1 lb. (454 g) corn sugar

HOPS

0.5 oz. (14 g) Magnum (US) (12% AA) @ 60 min.

0.5 oz. (14 g) Warrior (15% AA) @ 60 min.

0.25 oz. (7 g) Columbus (14% AA) @ 60 min.

0.25 oz. (7 g) Northern Brewer (US) (8.5% AA) @ 60 min.

0.5 oz. (14 g) Crystal (3.5% AA) @ 30 min.

0.25 oz. (7 g) Centennial (10% AA) @ 30 min.

0.25 oz. (7 g) Simcoe (13% AA) @ 30 min.

1.0 oz. (28 g) Amarillo (9.2% AA) @ 0 min.

2.0 oz. (56 g) Simcoe (13% AA) @ 5 days dry hop

2.0 oz. (56 g) Amarillo (9.2% AA) @ 5 days dry hop

ADDITIONAL INGREDIENTS

2.0–2.5 oz. (56–70 g) grapefruit peel strips (being careful only to peel the top
layer), retaining juice for marination

YEAST

White Labs California Ale Yeast WLP001

BREWING NOTES

Mash 60 min. @ 153°F (67°C).

Boil 60 min.

Ferment until terminal, then transfer to secondary.

Marinate grapefruit peel in its own juice for 24 hours to quasi-sterilize, then
remove, bag, and place in secondary.

Condition @ 35°F (2°C) 1 week until bright.

Carbonate to 2.5 volumes (4.9 g/L) CO_2.

IPA RECIPES WITH VEGETABLES

Cucumber Squeeze IPA *(For 5 US gallons [19 L])*

Cucumber Meyer Lemon IPA

Original gravity: 1.061 (15°P)
Final gravity: 1.010 (2.5°P)
Color: 3.9 SRM
Bitterness: 54 IBU
ABV: 6.7%

GRAIN BILL
95% 10.5 lb. (4.8 kg) Pilsner malt
5% 8 oz. (225 g) Weyermann Carahell malt

HOPS
1.7 oz. (48 g) CTZ* (15.5% AA) @ 90 min.
1.5 oz. (42 g) Citra (12% AA) @ 2 min.
0.5 oz. (14 g) Citra (12% AA) @ whirlpool

* A blend of Columbus, Tomahawk®, and Zeus.

ADDITIONAL INGREDIENTS
2 lb. (910 g) cucumbers
6 Meyer lemons

YEAST
Imperial Yeast A07 Flagship

BREWING NOTES

Wash and peel cucumbers. Puree flesh and retain for fermentation. Chop peels
  for mash.

Mash 60 min. @ 153°F (67°C) with cucumber peels (just for fun).

Zest or use a vegetable peeler to remove strips of peel from the Meyer lemons.

Boil 90 min., adding lemon peel to whirlpool.

Juice zested lemons.

Dilute cucumber puree with wort and reintroduce to fermentation vessel with
  the lemon juice.

Ferment until terminal, then transfer to secondary.

Condition @ 35°F (2°C) 1 week until bright.

Carbonate to 2.5 volumes (4.9 g/L) CO_2.

ADDITIONAL NOTES

A trick was once shown to me involving "de-bittering" a cucumber by
cutting off the end and rubbing it around the exposed area, drawing out the
white waxy stuff that is supposedly the bitter part of the peel. I have no idea
whether this works, or whether any of us would want to bother doing this
with so many cucumbers.

Fennelicious IPA *(For 5 US gallons [19 L])*

Fennel IPA

Original gravity: 1.064 (16°P)
Final gravity: 1.010 (2.5°P)
Color: 6.3 SRM
Bitterness: 52 IBU
ABV: 7.1%

GRAIN BILL

92% 12 lb. (5.5 kg) Great Western Malting Northwest Select 2-row malt

4% 8 oz. (225 g) Weyermann Munich malt

2% 4 oz. (112 g) Weyermann Carahell malt

2% 4 oz. (112 g) Crisp 70°L crystal malt

HOPS
4.6 oz. (130 g) Fuggle (US) (4.75% AA) @ 90 min.
1.5 oz. (42 g) German Northern Brewer (8.5% AA) @ 10 min.
0.5 oz. (14 g) German Northern Brewer (8.5% AA) @ 2 min.
0.5 oz. (14 g) German Northern Brewer (8.5% AA) @ whirlpool

ADDITIONAL INGREDIENTS
4 fennel bulbs with fronds

YEAST
Fuller's Yeast, or other attenuative English ale yeast

BREWING NOTES
Mash 60 min. @ 153°F (67°C).
Boil 90 min.
Chop and puree 4 fennel bulbs and stalks from whole plants, reserving fronds
    for whirlpool addition. Could also be juiced, for neater wort addition.
Add fronds to whirlpool.
Thin fennel puree (if used) with wort and reintroduce before pitching yeast.
Ferment until terminal, then transfer to secondary (optional addition of
    more fennel fronds in secondary).
Condition @ 35°F (2°C) 1 week until bright.
Carbonate to 2.5 volumes (4.9 g/L) CO_2.

ADDITIONAL NOTES
I like fennel fresh and juiced, but I also like it cooked, and it caramelizes well.
Go wild.

Maple Bardo IPA *(For 5 US gallons [19 L])*

Maple IPA

Thanks to Todd Boera of Fonta Flora Brewery, Morgantown, North Carolina and Fal Allen of Anderson Valley Brewing Company, Boonville, California for discussion about this recipe.

Original gravity: 1.065 (16.25°P)
Final gravity: 1.018 (4.5°P)
Color: 4.07 SRM
Bitterness: 57 IBU
ABV: 6.2%

GRAIN BILL
94% 11 lb. (5 kg) Great Western Malting Northwest Select 2-row malt
4% 8 oz. (225 g) Weyermann Munich malt
2% 4 oz. (112 g) Weyermann Carahell malt

HOPS
2 oz. (56 g) Centennial (10% AA) @ 90 min.
1.0 oz. (28 g) Galaxy (14% AA) @ 10 min.
1.0 oz. (28 g) Mosaic (12.25% AA) @ 2 min.
0.5 oz. (14 g) Simcoe (13% AA) @ whirlpool
0.5 oz. (14 g) Mosaic (12.25% AA) @ whirlpool
2.0 oz. (56 g) Galaxy (14% AA) @ dry hop (1 day before terminal)
2.0 oz. (56 g) Mosaic (12.25% AA) @ dry hop (1 day before terminal)

ADDITIONAL INGREDIENTS
1 lb. (454 g) maple syrup
1.0 oz. (28 g) roasted fenugreek seeds OR 0.02 oz. (0.5 g) candy cap
   mushroom powder

YEAST
Wyeast 1056

BREWING NOTES
Use maple sap for all brewing liquor, if seasonally and regionally feasible.
Mash 60 min. at 153°F (67°C).

Add maple syrup to wort (add an additional 2.5 oz. [70 g] if using straight
water as brewing liquor).

Boil 90 min.

Add fenugreek seeds or mushroom powder @ whirlpool.

Dry hop with Mosaic and Galaxy 1 day before terminal.

Ferment until terminal, then transfer to secondary.

Condition @ 35°F (2°C) 1 week until bright.

Carbonate to 2.5 volumes (4.9 g/L) CO_2.

ADDITIONAL NOTES

This beer would no doubt benefit from some contact with wood. Oak is
most readily available, of course, but it's fun to think about some contact
with maple.

Mr. McGregor's IPA *(For 5 US gallons [19 L])*

Ginger, Turmeric, Carrot, and Parsnip IPA

Original gravity: 1.064 (16°P)
Final gravity: 1.012 (3°P)
Color: 5.22 SRM (without vegetables)
Bitterness: 46 IBU
ABV: 6.8%

GRAIN BILL

93% 13 lb. (6 kg) Great Western Malting Northwest Select 2-row malt
3.5% 8 oz. (225 g) Weyermann Munich malt
1.75% 4 oz. (112 g) Weyermann Carahell malt
1.75% 4 oz. (112 g) Weyermann CaraVienne malt

HOPS

1.7 oz. (48 g) German Magnum (12% AA) @ 90 min.
1.0 oz. (28 g) Cascade (5.5% AA) @ 10 min.
1.0 oz. (28 g) Mandarina (8.5% AA) @ 10 min.
0.5 oz. (14 g) Cascade (5.5% AA) @ whirlpool
0.5 oz. (14 g) Mandarina (8.5% AA) @ whirlpool

ADDITIONAL INGREDIENTS
4 carrots, juiced
4 parsnips, juiced
2 oz. (56 g) ginger root, juiced
1.0 oz. (28 g) turmeric root, juiced

YEAST
Imperial Yeast A07 Flagship

BREWING NOTES
Mash 60 min. @ 153°F (67°C).
Boil 90 min.
Add juice mixture to fermentor.
Ferment until terminal, then transfer to secondary.
Condition @ 35°F (2°C) 1 week until bright.
Carbonate to 2.5 volumes (4.9 g/L) CO_2.

ADDITIONAL NOTES
Consider adding shredded carrot and parsnip (bagged) to conditioning
if flavor isn't bold enough. Avoid adding more juice at conditioning stage
because it is likely to ferment and render the beer unstable.

Jack o' Lupe IPA *(For 5 US gallons [19 L])*

Pumpkin Pineapple Sage IPA

Original gravity: 1.070 (16.5°P)
Final gravity: 1.020 (4.75°P)
Color: 9.89 SRM
Bitterness: 57 IBU
ABV: 6.6%

GRAIN BILL
85% 11 lb. (5 kg) American 2-row malt
8% 1 lb. (454 g) Weyermann Munich malt
4% 8 oz. (225g) Weyermann Dark Munich malt
2% 4 oz. (112 g) Weyermann Carahell malt
1% 2 oz. (56 g) Weyermann Carafa® II malt

HOPS

1.75 oz. (50 g) Columbus (14% AA) @ 90 min.
1.0 oz. (28 g) Mosaic (12.25% AA) @ 2 min.
1.0 oz. (28 g) Zythos (10.9% AA) @ 2 min.
1.5 oz. (42 g) Mosaic (12.25% AA) @ whirlpool
1.5 oz. (42 g) Zythos (10.9% AA) @ whirlpool

ADDITIONAL INGREDIENTS

8 oz. (225 g) unspiced pumpkin puree @ mash
8 oz. (225 g) unspiced pumpkin puree @ kettle
6 oz. (170 g) unspiced pumpkin puree @ fermentor
0.5 oz. (14 g) pineapple sage leaves

YEAST

Imperial Yeast A07 Flagship

BREWING NOTES

Mash 60 min. @ 153°F (67°C) with 8 oz. (225 g) pumpkin puree (thinned
   with water).
Boil 90 min. with 8 oz. (225 g) pumpkin puree (dilute with wort and
   reintroduce).
Add pineapple sage leaves @ whirlpool.
Ferment with 6 oz. (170 g) pumpkin puree (diluted with wort) until terminal,
   then transfer to secondary.
Condition @ 35°F (2°C) 1 week until bright.
Carbonate to 2.5 volumes (4.9 g/L) CO_2.

TABLE 3.1 LIST OF FRUITS AND THEIR ATTRIBUTES FOR USE IN BREWING IPAs

Fruit	Form(s)	Attributes	Combinations	Additions	Issues/Comments
Amchoor (mango powder)	Dried ground	Unripe mango, tart	Chili, ginger	Whirlpool, cold conditioning	Unripe mango quality could give nice tartness; also easy to use
Anardana (pomegranate seed)	Dried, whole or ground seeds	Pomegranate seeds	Fruity fill-in, tart	Hot infusion, then cold conditioning	Could be used with fruity hops or other actual fruit
Apple	Chopped, juiced	Sweet to tart	Nearly any non-citrus fruit, spices	Chopped or sauce to mash, juice to fermentor or at racking	Generically sweet flavor, often used for blends; tart varieties can add complexity; green apple quality could suggest acetaldehyde
Apricot	Fresh, pureed	Sweet/tart, depending on ripeness	Terpenic herbs, e.g., rosemary, thyme	Fermentation	Ties in with both esters and hop terpenes
Bergamot orange	Zest, juice, oil	Perfumy, orangey	Herbs, tea	Whirlpool, cold conditioning	Traditional addition for Earl Grey tea; a bit out there, but it works
Black lemon	Crushed or ground from whole dried fruit (lime)	Sweet/tart	Accent with citrus hops	Whirlpool, cold conditioning	Might be a nice fill-in or counterpoint kind of thing with aroma hops
Blackberry	Whole or pureed	Fragrant/perfumey, sweet/tart, color	Terpenic herbs, other berries	Fermentation	Plenty of precedent, but over-sweet treatment risks compromise of style
Blueberry	Whole or pureed	Quiet fragrance, slight blush of color	Other berries, but generally avoiding strong flavor	Fermentation, cold conditioning	Very mild flavor and effect, including color
Buddha's hand	Chopped, juiced	Very tart and lemony	Hops, but very bitter itself	Cold conditioning	Intensely bitter and tart, get used to it solo first
Carob	Meal, powder, or syrup	Waxy, mild sweetness, tannin	Theoretically, where chocolate might otherwise be used	Powder in whirlpool, meal in secondary/conditioning, syrup in fermentation or later on the cold side	An unhappy substitute for chocolate or cocoa, with all its fatty pitfalls; even Wikipedia cites one of its best uses as "chocolate" treats for dogs

Fruit	Form(s)	Attributes	Combinations	Additions	Issues/Comments
Cashew fruit (cajú)	Whole	Subtle nuttiness, hint of soap	Sour treatment	Cold conditioning, in barrel	The red and yellow fruit appended to the cashew nut, extremely perishable
Cherry (sour)	Whole or pureed	Tartness, with deep cherry flavor	Hop bitterness, fruity esters	Fermentation, or more likely secondary/conditioning	Judicious use in IPA can be a nice touch, as long as cherry flavor is kept mild enough to allow malt/ester/hop flavors to shine through
Cherry (sweet)	Whole or pureed	Sweetness and cherry flavor	Fruity esters, hop flavor	Fermentation, or more likely secondary/conditioning	Don't allow to make beer too sweet, but could provide a nice touch of flavor
Citron	Zest or juice	Tartness and a very thick peel	Citrusy hops, other citrus fruit	Whirlpool (peel) or fermentation (juice)	The etrog ("beautiful fruit") employed in Sukkot ritual
Coconut	Shredded	Tropical depth and possible waxiness	Tropical-effect hops (NZ, Australia, Japan), e.g., Sorachi Ace; wood aging	Mash, whirlpool, fermentation, or cold side/conditioning	Oils can challenge head retention; don't overdo it, but can provide nice counterpoint to barrel aging and fermentation esters
Currants (red, black, white)	Crushed fresh	Tart and bright	Sour treatments	Fermentation, cold conditioning	Many colors and varieties, tart to fully/ripely sweet
Damson	Whole or pureed	Tartness and tannin from skins and pits	Fruity esters and fruity hop varieties; citrus, or other stone fruit	Fermentation, or more likely secondary/conditioning	Tartness can provide good counterpoint to hop flavors and esters
Date	Chopped or syrup	Sugary, dried fruit effect; syrup is very sweet	Malt backbone, esters, contrast with hop characters	Chopped or syrup to fermentation, syrup to conditioning	Can provide nice depth of flavor; be careful using syrup, it is very sweet and dense and needs lots of agitation

Table 3.1 continued on next page

TABLE 3.1 (cont.)

Fruit	Form(s)	Attributes	Combinations	Additions	Issues/Comments
Dragon fruit	Peeled, chopped and pureed	Mild tropical fruit flavor, colored varieties provide color—others not so much, peel color notwithstanding	Other tropical fruits and kiwis	Fermentation, cold conditioning	Beautiful pink exterior often belies grayish, seedy interior; very mild flavor effect for inevitable expense; pink-fleshed varieties do give nice color
Durian	Chopped, pureed	Very funky flavor and aroma, intense	Perhaps other tropical fruits, but so strong that it should perhaps be unleashed only with intense hops, and in combination with fermentation esters	Fermentation, cold conditioning	A double-edged sword; very unpleasantly fragrant—there's a reason they are illegal to carry on public transportation throughout Southeast Asia; an acquired taste, and a very nervy specialty use
Fig	Chopped, pureed	Tart to sweet, depending on ripeness; also varies whether pale or dark variety	Pale types—hops, grapes, gooseberries; dark types—esters, other malt character, plums or raisins	Fermentation, cold conditioning	Depending on variety, could combine with different sides of IPA character—brighter, fruity-hop character (pale), malty base, other darker fruit (dark)
Grape	Crushed, pureed	Tart to sweet, depending on ripeness and variety	Hops, honey	Fermentation, cold conditioning	An underused element, can provide complexity and sharp, fruity tie-in; wild yeasts could also give complexity
Grapefruit	Zested, peeled, juiced, or concentrate	Aroma, flavor, bitterness	Hops, other citrus	Mash, fermentation, cold conditioning, in keg (zest in particular)	Entry-level fruit tie-in with hops, versatile and bold
Guava	Pureed	Aroma, sourness, tartness	Tropical hops, terpenic herbs, chilies	Fermentation, cold conditioning	Lovely, tart tropical flavor and aroma
Jackfruit	Chopped, pureed	See Durian	See Durian	Fermentation, cold conditioning	See Durian, though larger in raw form

Fruit	Form(s)	Attributes	Combinations	Additions	Issues/Comments
Kabosu	Juice	Melony effect amid semi-tart citrus	Guava, tamarind, kiwi, berries	Fermentation, cold conditioning	Taste alongside yuzu and sudachi for contrast
Kiwi fruit	Pureed, juiced	Melony sweetness if ripe, tart if unripe	Tropical hop or fruity North American hop varieties; esters; other fruits, e.g., grape, melon, gooseberries	Fermentation, cold conditioning	Seedy and with a tenacious peel—a masticating juicer will extract both, but will take time
Kumquat	Chopped, pureed	Citrusy bite, some sweetness	Chilies, terpenic herbs, chocolate	Fermentation, cold conditioning	Another secret weapon, good balance of sweet and tart to meld with malt and hops
Lemon	Zested, peeled, juiced, or concentrate	Citrus oil, juicy	Other citrus, ginger, terpenic herbs	Fermentation, cold conditioning, racking	Ties in well with hops; combination of peel and juice a strong addition
Lime	Zested, peeled, juiced, or concentrate	Citrus oil, juicy	Other citrus, tamarind, mango	Fermentation, cold conditioning, racking	Ties in well with hops, but also accompanies other things tropical
Longan	Peeled, seeded, or pureed	Waxy, tart	Lime, other citrus	Fermentation, cold conditioning	Similar to lychee (also rambutan), but not as aromatic
Loquat	Peeled, seeded, or pureed	Flavor like mango and peach	Tropical and fruity hops	Fermentation, cold conditioning	Tart and flavorful when ripe, but must be peeled and seeded
Lulo (naranjilla)	Fresh, concentrate	Rhubarb/lime, a bit pasty	Tropical, piney, and fruity hops; berries	Fermentation, cold conditioning	Name is from Quechua, also known as naranjilla, of the nightshade family, looks like persimmon
Lychee	Peeled and pureed	Tart and aromatic	Tropical and fruity hops	Fermentation, cold conditioning	Perfumy and aromatic

Table 3.1 continued on next page

TABLE 3.1 (cont.)

Fruit	Form(s)	Attributes	Combinations	Additions	Issues/Comments
Mango	Pureed	Sweet, with distinctive tartness when ripe; very tart when underripe, but still delicious	Anything tropical—fruit or hops	Fermentation, cold conditioning	Degree of ripeness key to effect
Meyer lemon	Zested, peeled, juiced, concentrate	Sweet/tart hybrid, far sweeter than regular lemon	Ginger, vanilla, turmeric, pomegranate, pink peppercorn	Fermentation, cold conditioning, racking	Versatile and distinctive, combines well due to relative lack of citrus intensity
Nectarine	Pureed	Fragrant and tart, like peach but different	Vanilla, cinnamon, thyme, evergreen tips	Fermentation, cold conditioning	A natural combined with hops
Orange	Zested, peeled, juiced, concentrate	Sweet to tart to oily to intense	Spice, chocolate, coffee, terpenic herbs	Fermentation, cold conditioning, racking	Balance particularly important due to potential sweetness
Blood orange	Zested, peeled, juiced, concentrate	Tart, nice blush of color	Bold North American hops	Fermentation, cold conditioning, racking	Fashionably exotic, therefore somewhat difficult to source
Mandarin	Zested, peeled, juiced, concentrate	Different varieties offer subtle varieties of flavor and tartness	Probably stand-alone due to subtlety and sweetness	Fermentation, cold conditioning, racking	Several varieties; very juicy; peel more difficult to work with than stiffer, conventional oranges
Orange (sweet orange)	Zested, peeled, juiced, concentrate	Plainly sweet, oily	Cascade hops	Fermentation, cold conditioning, racking	Simple, easily obtained
Seville orange (bitter orange)	Zested, peeled, juiced, concentrate	Surprisingly bitter	Malt sweetness can balance orange bitterness	Fermentation, cold conditioning, racking	Run some taste experiments before you commit
Papaya	Peeled, seeded, pureed	Varies greatly as to ripeness, tart and green to lush and funky	Other tropical fruits; Slovenian hops	Fermentation, cold conditioning	Versatile; shredded green could be a nice mash addition too; pulped or pureed ripe for fermentation; green again in conditioning

Fruit	Form(s)	Attributes	Combinations	Additions	Issues/Comments
Passion fruit	Peeled, seeded, pureed	Haunting tartness	NZ hops; terpenic herbs	Fermentation, cold conditioning	A natural for fruit IPAs
Pawpaw (Asimina triloba)	Scooped from skin, separated from seeds	Custardy and somewhat fibrous	Dextrine malt (for texture), chocolate	Fermentation	Seed and peel need to be negotiated
Peach	Pureed, concentrate	Fragrant and tart; like nectarine only different	Spices, vanilla, thyme; fruity hops	Fermentation (including concentrate during later stages of fermentation), cold conditioning	Local varieties, e.g., Yakima, Palisade, and Georgia, make for an excellent seasonal IPA
Pear	Pureed, juiced, concentrate	Ranges from woody to cloying; lots of varieties to choose from	Herbs and mints, root vegetables, fennel	Fermentation, cold conditioning, racking	Less appley varieties probably most appropriate, a touch with European or NZ hops
Asian pear	Pureed, juiced	Sweet and surprisingly juicy, not complex	Plum; Asian spices	Fermentation, cold conditioning	Big and juicy; more complex when less ripe
European pear	Pureed, juiced	Many varieties, tart and sweet	Herbs, hops, rose	Fermentation, cold conditioning	Use varieties distinct from apples to avoid acetaldehyde association
Persimmon	Pureed	Puckery when unripe, tart and compelling when ripe—check variety	Hops	Fermentation	Taste before you use—you won't believe how dry unripe ones can make your mouth; a natural for IPA and hop complexity
Pineapple	Pureed, juiced	Quintessentially tropical	Chilies, terpenic herbs, other tropical fruits	Fermentation, cold conditioning	Don't overdo it; can tie in nicely with certain hops
Plum	Pureed	Many varieties, tart and sweet	Shiso, thyme, salt, hops	Fermentation	Excellent with hops

Table 3.1 continued on next page

TABLE 3.1 (cont.)

Fruit	Form(s)	Attributes	Combinations	Additions	Issues/Comments
Pomegranate	Juiced, molasses	Tartness, color	Flowers and teas	Fermentation, cold conditioning	Molasses is ponderously thick and syrupy—agitate well and repeatedly or you will regret it, as it stratifies easily and decisively
Pomelo	Zested, peeled, juiced, concentrate	Aroma, flavor, bitterness	Hops, honey	Fermentation, cold conditioning	Like grapefruit, only different
Prickly pear	Peeled and pureed	Range of colors—pink ones give a nice color, some tart sharpness	Strong-flavored honey, sour treatments	Fermentation, cold conditioning	Good regional (or exotic) touch
Quince	Pureed, juiced	Tart and unique	Other fruits such as pomegranate and cactus; herbs	Fermentation, cold conditioning	As different from pear as pear is from apple—interesting
Sloe	Pureed, juiced, cooked	Plummy, cherry-like	Other stone fruits, terpenic herbs, evergreen	Fermentation	Gives nice touch of the forager; occupies indefinible middle ground
Star fruit	Pureed, juiced	Tart and citrus-like	Herbs, hops	Fermentation, cold conditioning	Strong flavor, nice with fruity hops
Sudachi	Juice	Black pepper on top of citrus	Tropical fruits and hops; chilies	Fermentation, cold conditioning	Another Japanese citrus fruit
Tamarillo	Peeled, seeded, pureed	Tart and guava-like	Herbs, hops, kiwi, cactus	Fermentation, cold conditioning	Not aware of commercial purees, so you're on your own; can be unique and wonderful in IPA
Tamarind	Crushed and strained, liquid or reconstituted	The indefinibly tart flavor in pad thai	Hops, herbs, limes	Fermentation	Earthy tartness calls out for consideration with hop varieties
Tangerine	Zested, peeled, juiced, concentrate	Uniquely citrusy, with variants	Herbs, hops	Fermentation, cold conditioning	A natural for fruit IPAs
Yuzu	Zested, peeled, juiced, concentrate	Lime-tangerine citrusy	Shiso, plums, other citrus, phenols	Fermentation, cold conditioning	Fresh form doesn't yield much juice; commercially available juice more reliable

TABLE 3.2 LIST OF VEGETABLES AND THEIR ATTRIBUTES FOR USE IN BREWING IPAs

Vegetable	Form(s)	Attributes	Combinations	Additions	Issues/Comments
Asparagus	Raw pureed, cooked pureed	Earthy, "green," pea-like	Lemon, pepper	Mash, fermentor	Distinctive and strong aroma and flavor; perhaps at odds with bitterness
Beet	Raw pureed, cooked pureed, juiced	Earthy, metallic, sweet	Other root vegetables, white pepper, rosemary, evergreen	Fermentor, cold conditioning	Strong earthy and metallic flavor; interesting color(s)
Carrot	Raw pureed, cooked pureed, juiced	Bright, sugary, caramel (cooked)	Ginger, celery, chili, herbs	Fermentor, cold conditioning	Sugary, caramelizes well
Celeriac	Raw chopped or shredded	Sharp, herbal, peppery	Carrot, celery seed	Mash, cold conditioning	An earthy touch
Celery	Raw pureed, cooked pureed, juiced	Earthy-herbal	Carrot, almond	Fermentor, cold conditioning	Probably not, especially if cooked
Cucumber	Raw peeled, shredded or pureed	Lightly sharp, white peppery	Dill, white pepper, lemon	Peels in mash; puree in fermentor	Watery, leaves a hint of flavor when fermented
Dandelion	Raw shredded or pureed	Bitter, peppery	Radish, parsnip	Mash, fermentor, cold conditioning	Could work well with hop bitterness
Endive	Raw chopped, shredded, or pureed; cooked	Bitter, peppery	Cinnamon, carrot	Mash, fermentor	Very bitter, slightly cabbagey when cooked
Fennel	Raw chopped; cooked caramelized and pureed	Anise	Hops, carrot	Greens in mash; pureed bulbs and stalks in fermentor	Can be nice combination with specific Continental hops, e.g., German Northern Brewer
Fiddlehead	Raw chopped, cooked chopped	Earthy, spring-bright	Mushroom, endive	Mash, fermentor	Conceptual vernal touch, combine with other seasonal stuff

Table 3.2 continued on next page

TABLE 3.2 (cont.)

Vegetable	Form(s)	Attributes	Combinations	Additions	Issues/Comments
Greens	Raw chopped or juiced	Peppery, cabbagey	Beets and carrots in combination with their roots	Fermentor, cold conditioning	Be careful
Horseradish	Raw shredded	Hot	Caraway	Mash, cold conditioning	Slight addition could provide quiet back note to hop aroma
Mushroom	Shredded in alcoholic tincture	Earthy, complex	Root vegetables	Cold conditioning, racking	An odd choice for IPA, works with malt sugar and fruity esters in other pale ales
Nettle	Cooked and pureed	Sharp, herbal, peppery	Mushrooms, other foraged stuff	Mash, fermentor, cold conditioning	Noxious and irritating unless cooked
Onions	Raw flowers, shredded greens	Strong, sharp	Greens or flowers with IPA or an infusion, otherwise probably avoid	Mash	Probably a bad idea, but a floral touch could tie in with hops
Parsley	Raw whole or chopped	Herbal, bright	Carrot, parsnip, sweet pepper	Mash, fermentor, cold conditioning	Accent only
Parsnip	Raw pureed, cooked pureed, juiced	Spicy, peppery, bright	Carrot, beet, shiso	Mash, fermentor	Could add intriguing earthy spiciness
Peppers, sweet	Raw pureed, roasted pureed	Sugary, caramel (if cooked)	Carrot, onion greens, thyme/mint herbs	Mash, fermentor, cold conditioning	With a sharp accompaniment could provide a nice accent to a bitter beer
Peppers, hot	Raw chopped	Spicy-hot	Make fruit salsa—peach, nectarine	Mash, fermentor, cold conditioning	Work with hops; don't forget their touch of sweetness
Pumpkin	Raw pureed, cooked pureed	Earthy, slippery mouthfeel, astringency	Spices, herbs, souring	Mash, kettle, fermentor	Recommend more aroma than bitterness in hopping
Radish	Raw shredded or pureed	Hot, earthy	Watercress, caraway	Mash, cold conditioning	A bold move

Vegetable	Form(s)	Attributes	Combinations	Additions	Issues/Comments
Rhubarb	Raw pureed, cooked pureed, juiced	Tart and distinctive, also color	Strawberry (duh), apple, ginger, turmeric, mint	Fermentor, cold conditioning	A fruity vegetable secret weapon, complex and compelling
Seaweed	Steeped in brewing liquor (dashi), shredded (dulse, kelp)	Slick mouthfeel, briny touch	Peppers, grapes, seawater	Brewing liquor, mash, cold conditioning	Evocative of coastal areas (like Islay whisky)
Squash	Raw pureed, cooked pureed	Bright and earthy (raw), caramel (cooked)	Spices, sour treatments	Fermentor	See Pumpkin
Sweet potato / yam	Cooked pureed	Earthy, sweet	Peppers, parsnip	Mash, fermentor	See Pumpkin
Tomatillo	Raw pureed	Sharp	Chili, citrus	Fermentor	Sharp accent could tie in with hop bitterness
Watercress	Raw chopped or pureed	Peppery	Carrot, celery, horseradish	Mash, fermentor, cold conditioning	Minced and cold-infused could give a nice note
Zucchini	Raw pureed, cooked pureed	Watery (raw); caramel (cooked)	Onion flower, carrot, pumpkin	Fermentor	Not a strong flavor alone

4

TIME AND PLACE, HERB AND SPICE

It's well known that the use of herbs and spices in beer predates the use of hops, and that the somewhat confusing delineation of beer and ale once differentiated beverages made with and without the use of hops, respectively. Once hops took hold, in fact, spices and herbs were left largely to languish where brewing was concerned, continuing mainly as flavorings for food and in medicines, but appearing in beer only here and there. We also know that the issue was politically, economically, and even religiously charged, with the rights to taxes paid on herbal gruit mixtures often held by the church, which represented a meaningful income to itself but an onerous expense to brewers. Little wonder that once hops appeared they brought with them a disincentive for continuing to use these other flavorings, and especially as people seemed generally to like hopped beer. Struggles ensued, along with conflicts, excommunications, and embargoes. In Germany, with the adoption of the *Reinheitsgebot* in 1516, the use of any materials other than malted barley, hops, and water became explicitly illegal. (In its modern form, the *Reinheitsgebot* obviously includes yeast and, for some types of beer, other malted grains such as wheat.) This included spices and herbs, of course, but also pretty much everything else we consider in this book. Should they have existed back then, one has to wonder if an addendum might have been drafted to additionally prohibit Cascade, Motueka, and other hops perhaps regarded as exotic, given that they weren't grown in Bavaria. Maybe that's just being snarky.

Let's just say it's a good thing we can use what we want in beer, including herbs and spices, without the church or the government making it their business (mostly). In this chapter, we'll at least consider a little transgression as well.

I'm guessing that most cities of some size have a decent spice market. Seattle, Washington does, and I'm not talking about the chain stores, good in their own way as an alternative to the five or six feet of aisle space devoted to spices in a typical grocery store or supermarket, but still a far cry from a real spice market with the feel of a local bazaar. I will hammer just a bit on those chain stores, since much of what they sell is spice mixes, be it curry powder, chili powder, or maybe mixed mole spices, for example. These store-bought mixes can be well-crafted and serviceable, but they are shortcuts, combining things in a way their professionals have justly deemed delicious but taking any possibility for customization away from the consumer. For many people that's just fine (and I've got some of their stuff in my cupboard, too, for when I don't want to do all that grinding), but it's like using malt extract for brewing—the results can be delicious, but all the choices have been made for you in the interests of ease, consistency, and saving time. Please don't even consider the supermarket. The herbs and spices for sale there are strictly for emergencies, like when you've got dinner underway and realize you're out of fennel seed. They're also, ounce for ounce, generally a lot more expensive. These days, of course, and for those who might not have a local spice market of quality, there are excellent online options too. The only problem there is that you can't sniff and taste things in person.

Just walking into my local spice market gives me ideas of things to add to beer, even if I don't yet have any idea what that beer would be. It makes me want to build a beer around things like Balinese long pepper and Vietnamese cinnamon, and maybe to twist in the accent of some other obscure pepper. But however interesting and diverting that may be, it isn't what we're here now to do. We're taking a beer type that, with some variation, is well established as to style and attributes and we're coming up with things that will harmonize with and play off of hops, esters, malty sweetness, the possibly phenolic qualities of yeast, and maybe, in some cases, the foodiness of oak. With that understanding, we can still take that walk around the bazaar, sticking our noses into the display jars and considering what we might hazard a dash or two of in our IPA.

Herbs and spices are evocative, conjuring places and their cuisines; they can also speak across time, retracing the trade routes of yore, the exploration of new lands and the subsumption of cooking culture and agriculture. How a European herb such as cilantro made it across the world to become a staple of southeast Asian cooking is just one example. Jamaican allspice is the predominant flavor of jerk chicken, ground sassafras leaves form the uniquely flavored filé used in gumbo, but neither is probably going to combine well with the boldness of IPA, unless perhaps to push a conceptual point. But deconstruct the curry powder that trumpets Indian cuisine and you might be onto something. Indian curries, of course, vary widely according to where they arise and the spice mixes that go into them. Most have the signature of yellow turmeric; many also have cardamom, clove, coriander, cinnamon, cumin, ginger, fenugreek, or black pepper, among others and in various combinations. One or two of those ingredients may combine nicely with the spiciness or fruity sharpness of hops or the roastiness of malt to make a delicious and beguiling IPA with a nice conceptual link to the land forever linked with its story. And let's not forget that there are curries from other lands as well. More than the fruits and vegetables we've already examined in the previous chapter, herbs and spices, especially spices, tell a story simply by their presence. And I've always said every beer has a story.

Distilling is not a cuisine as such, but inspiration can also be taken from herbal and botanical mixtures used to flavor bitter and aromatic liqueurs, aperitifs, and digestifs. Gin in particular sets a collective example of variety, incorporating proprietary blends of spices, herbs, and botanicals, including not just the juniper berries with which everyone is familiar, but also cassia, cubeb berries, citrus peel, coriander, orris root, angelica, and grains of paradise, among others. Working closely with a friendly distiller offers a great cross-branding opportunity, especially if you age your IPA in their gin barrels—Beer Street and Gin Lane all in one, without the Hogarthian judgement.

HERBS IN IPA

Are You Going To Scarborough Fair?

Among specialty ingredients, herbs are probably most commonly and obviously used in adding to an IPA. Terpenic tie-ins (see appendix) are evident with rosemary, thyme, oregano, shiso, basil, and others; but while their use can be conceptually justified by the fact that the same compounds variously turn up in specific hop varieties, discretion must be used. Tying in can be tantamount to tying up, dominating the flavor of a beer with something that might be more appropriate as a background note, or that isn't appropriate at all. Basil, for example, strikes me as too sweetly flavored to be more than subtly worked into the herbal sharpness and already sweet maltiness that an IPA has as its constituent parts. Shiso too is pretty bold. Italian oregano seems a little too food-like, perhaps, unfairly, suggesting marinara; but make that oregano Mexican, or bring in epazote, or even some of that shiso after all, and you're talking creosote and resin to walk alongside the appropriate hop. Of this list, I think rosemary is best of all, piney and a bit harsh, like a lot of Northwest hops; and speaking of which, it grows like a weed throughout much of western IPA-land.

Speaking of growing things, herbs are perhaps the most appropriate and gratifying of all the ingredients we're liable to deal with. They are easy to plant and tend, and lend themselves to combinations in both cooking and augmenting the flavors of beer. They can also be a pleasantly aromatic presence outside your kitchen or brewery window. Given the space necessary—and space can often be appropriated on rooftops and in other odd spots—a brewery herb garden can be just the thing for seasonally generating (and preserving through drying into other times of year) an array of flavors for use in concert with the bold hop character of IPA, and for other beers besides.

Trees themselves can provide interesting, herbally-aligned flavorings for beer. The springtime tips of regenerating spruce, pine, or fir can add a spicy, sappy note to any beer, and in IPA that can work with aroma and flavor hops in resinous harmony. The pale green tips of spruce can be added late on the hot side (e.g., in the whirlpool) or bagged and added on the cold side to give a spicy, cola-like flavor. Maple too can be used to make an interestingly flavored IPA, with unconcentrated sap (where available) used as brewing liquor or syrup added to fermentation. Juniper bushes are useful beyond the berries used to flavor gin; the branches of common juniper can be added to brewing liquor or the mash to flavor wort, and can also be steam-sterilized and hung in the conditioning tank during the aging process. For every caution where the ingestion of juniper is concerned there is a corresponding theoretical benefit; still, with the variety of types growing ornamentally throughout the world, it's best to identify the variety and read up just a bit before use. This would apply as well to evergreen tips—remember Socrates and hemlock.

Roughly speaking, herbs are typically classified as culinary, aromatic, or those used to make tea by infusion. On the surface, herbs are not unlike different hop varieties in being optimal for a particular assignment, be it bittering, flavor, or aroma; but, offhand, I'd say there's greater difference between sage and lemon verbena, for example, than among most hop varieties (hop-headed taxonomists might disagree).

Culinary herbs, in addition to the rosemary, thyme, oregano, shiso, and basil already mentioned, includes such herbs as chervil, mint, borage, parsley, and chives. Chives are liable to carry the off flavors of onion; parsley, like oregano, to connote food rather too much; but the cucumbery note of borage could bring an intriguing zest alongside a citrusy hop variety or actual lemon.

The herbal combinations we employ in cooking, of course, can inform choices we make when crafting recipes for beer.

Aromatic herbs need to be employed in IPA and other beer with special care, for to overdo them can result in something one might as well call "Grandma's IPA." There are stores and websites devoted to creating various herbal mixtures for potpourri, and this is what your beer will taste like if you combine too many of these essentially floral aromas into a single entity. Still, a note of rose, violet, sweet woodruff, or bergamot could be managed. Perhaps conceptually, as with spice mixes such as curry or mole, all that floral combination needs some deconstruction. It's also to be noted that some aromas are polarizing, possibly dividing even more sharply than usual those loving and those hating a particular beer. I have experienced this in the past with lavender—to some a lovely and ethereal note, to others just plain soap.

The herbs ordinarily used for making tea may be those with the greatest applicability for augmenting IPA, especially given that hops themselves are often listed as belonging to this group. Some, such as chamomile, lovage, and caraway are particularly strongly flavored and would likely dominate any beer in which they were incorporated; with them I'd counsel a combination of courage and discretion. Others such as heather could add a light, geographically evocative note. Fennel, with its anise essence, is an obvious tie-in with some hop varieties such as Northern Brewer or Centennial, which could meet it symbiotically halfway. Some other flowers such as jasmine and calendula do double duty as aromatics and in tea, and they too can be pleasingly yoked to earthy and floral hop aromas. Whether it is to be classified as herbal or not, actual tea is a fun element to consider as well. We will examine this more closely in chapter 5, which treats the use of coffee in IPA.

Herbs, spices, and teas of all types tend to be dried for shipping, stability, and effectiveness. Some of the culinary herbs, such as mint, thyme, chives, parsley, and dill are often most effective fresh (though they too are dried), while others are frequently cooked in order to unlock their flavors. Many, such as tarragon and oregano literally multiply in effect when dried; similarly, sweet woodruff is benign and grassy when fresh, cinnamon and vanilla-like when laid out for a couple of days. Aromatic herbs are typically dried to maximize their floral qualities, and like delicate noble hops used for finishing beer, would become subdued to nothing if boiled overmuch, or even protractedly steeped. Others, including floral and herbal teas and spices, depend on the dispersal of their flavors and character by infusion in hot liquid, and otherwise provide no more aromatic addition than a handful of hay.

Avatar Jasmine IPA—an Herbal Incarnation

It was in 1995 (I think), my first GABF judging panel ever, and I don't think I said a word the whole time. By the end of the day I would have loosened up sufficiently to get into a mild argument about Märzen with George Fix, author of *Principles of Brewing Science* and the Brewers Publications *Classic Beer Styles Series* title on Oktoberfest, without, of course, realizing who he was at the time; but, on that first morning, I was awed by the company in which I sat. I'd love to see a complete list of who it was that so daunted me, but I do remember Steve Parkes, who then worked at Humboldt Brews in Arcata, California, and Fred Eckhardt, the Portland *Oregonian* columnist and Rushmorian figure in our movement. I mainly remember Fred, whom at that point I vaguely knew through Northwestern circles, because partway through the round, as we were sipping and studiously scribbling, he broke into improvised song. "IPA," he sang, to no particular tune, "My little IPA . . ."

Also on the panel was a fellow who would later become quite a good friend, Mark Dorber, who in those days managed the legendary White Horse pub in Parsons Green in London, well known for bringing craft beer and brewing culture from all over the world to the attention of the stylish crowds that nightly filled "The Sloaney Pony." Mark's was also a dependable and patient voice in teaching all of us—and, by extension, I mean all of us—about cask-conditioned beer and the techniques of cellarmanship to keep it in proper trim. He brought young people from throughout the world, including one of my own charges at Elysian, to work at the White Horse, behind the bar and in the cellar, and by so doing I believe helped sow the seeds of revolution now bearing more mainstream, craft-beer-appreciative fruit across Europe and beyond.

One of the IPAs we tasted in that first-round session particularly impressed Mark, and not because it displayed the tongue-napalming intensity of the fierce IPAs with which we are today familiar, or even the genie of hop aroma that can fill rooms as effectively as the perfume of night-blooming cereus. These were the days, remember, before there was even a subcategory of IPA tolerant of American hops. No, for Mark it was a subtler sensory message, with a fairly low-profile descriptor: "This beer really reminds me of jasmine tea," he offered more than once, "I love it."

Well, this isn't that kind of Cinderella story. None of the rest of the panelists were as impressed as Mark by the floral-herbal hop aroma he described (or maybe even failed to pick it up)—I honestly don't remember much more of that discussion. The beer didn't make it out of the first round that year, but Mark's impression did stick in my mind. It struck me that the addition of actual jasmine to an IPA might make for an interesting beer. It took me several years to do it, as it happened, and not until I had moved on from the job at Big Time Brewery that I held then, started my own brewery, and then opened a second, satellite location with a low-stakes three-barrel brewery that could be kept in a mostly out-of-the-way back room.

What I built as a base beer was an IPA with some of its excesses tamed, to give more play to the jasmine I intended to add at a couple of stages during late hopping. It was less strong than our flagship IPA at the time, less fiercely and distinctively hoppy, but pretty much down the line where pale beers with mostly non-invasive specialty malts live in the recipe file of one's mind. I had ordered dried jasmine flowers from an outfit in San Francisco, and hung a bag of them in the kettle for about the last ten minutes of the boil, and then another once the flame had been struck and the too-fast whirlpool spun the contents of the kettle. If nothing else, I was onto something redolent. Jasmine aroma filled the room and the neighborhood, and when the beer was ready a mild grapiness also played among its flavors. Some weeks later we found that we had reached a generally non-IPA demographic—women—when at our biggest local summer beer festival we had a long line of people waiting for the beer, many of them women bringing their husbands and boyfriends to try the beer they had already had and enjoyed.

There's more to the story of Elysian Avatar Jasmine IPA, but none of it is as important as its inspiration and initial creation. There was the time, when brewing a 20-barrel batch and having secured the bags of jasmine in the kettle with lightish-gauge wire and soon after hearing the pings of its severing, I had to descend into the emptied but still hot kettle (attempting to breathe through a length of beverage tubing) to retrieve the jasmine bags for dunking in the whirlpool. There was the time my jasmine source temporarily dried up and I unwittingly bought, and later had to dispose of, 500 pounds of thoroughly un-aromatic flowers. There were the Band-Aids and bullets that a contractor operating the hammer mill found in a batch of jasmine from China. And there were medals from both the GABF and WBC. There's even more, such as when I walked into the White Horse several years later and found an English copycat version (brewed by another friend) dispensed from one of the hand pumps, thereby closing the circle. Every beer, as I've often said and will no doubt continue to say, has a story.

Articles of Incorporation—"Herb" in IPA

Many of us have over the years noticed the aromatic congruence between marijuana and hops, and, of course, it has been pointed out that the two plants are taxonomically closely related and some of the physical properties of tetrahydrocannabinol (THC) and alpha acids are similar. The naming and packaging of many IPAs has winkingly alluded as much, with words such as "dank" and "herbacious" often used by brewers and their waitstaff to describe beers made with hop varieties particularly evocative of pot. Weed-related descriptors are often used to describe the properties of specific hop varieties, even at a corporate level.

Much of this speculation and (previously) extra-legal experimentation has since been dispensed with, because, as of this writing, around 20% of the US population lives in states (and Washington, DC) where recreational use of marijuana has been legalized. Even in these places, the use of cannabis-related products by professional brewers has been limited to hemp seeds and essences of cannabidiol (CBD), typically introduced on the cold side and without psychoactive effect, this having to do with the fact that these brewers hold federal licenses and so are prohibited from having THC show up in their beer. Homebrewers in these appropriately enlightened states, however, are free to brew beers that make use of all properties of marijuana. It's parenthetically interesting, in fact, to note that these same states are those in which small-scale brewing took earliest popular hold, but that's as far as our half-"baked" demographic analysis will go.

In any case, the strong flavors of IPA lend themselves well, should one be so inclined, to the introduction of marijuana for both flavor and effect. This presents a couple of logistical challenges. It's well known amid circles of hempen aficionados that for THC to be incorporated effectively into any medium intended for ingestion and subsequent psychoactive effect some solubilizing medium is required, typically fat or ethanol. This is why such treats are often baked, which binds active THC to digestible oil or butter, as well as introducing strong flavors such as chocolate to mitigate harsh flavors. But if ever there was a beer style appropriate in its other excesses to accommodate the flavors and other properties of marijuana, it is certainly IPA. (Hops too, of course, need to be hot-infused in order to contribute bitterness.)

The ethanol option might seem to be taken care of given the alcoholic component of beer, but while technically present, the alcoholic concentration in even a strong IPA is not nearly as effective as a tincture made using stronger spirits such as vodka or the more neutral Everclear®. It's surprising, in fact, to note that such a venerable oracle of things weed-related as *High Times* referenced a recipe seeming to ignore the facts of THC assimilation, calling it good with a hot side whirlpool addition and later, cold side "dry potting," further claiming that a single 12-ounce bottle of homebrew would carry the same effect as a brownie (McDonough 2016).

Possibly more effective and interesting as a medium is lightly heated olive oil. This might on the surface seem anathema, given the head-killing property of other fats in beer. But combine that treated olive oil with active yeast slurry and an extra mycologically nutritive benefit is gained. This shows that the subject could be further explored, but for now I will simply refer the reader to the "Steal This Beer" sidebar and to further reading in the bibliography (Andre et al. 2016; Sorini and Burrows 2017; Sumpson 2014).

Steal This Beer—Infusing IPA with Cannabis

As of this writing, approximately 20% of the US population live in places in which recreational use of cannabis products is legal. This means, by extension, that in these places it's also legal to introduce such things into beer. But only for homebrewers. I'll say that again: *only for homebrewers.* Professional brewers, while licensed for operation and sale in their home states, are also required to hold a license with the Alcohol and Tobacco Tax and Trade Bureau (TTB), an agency of the US Department of the Treasury. As an instrument of federal law, this license prohibits the introduction of any substance not approved for use by TTB. Since intoxicating cannabis is explicitly illegal at the federal level, but grudgingly allowed by the federal government in those states (and the District of Columbia) where it has been voted and legislated to be legal, any licensed brewer in the United States who added cannabis products containing THC (the psychoactive constituent in marijuana and hashish) to a beer and offered it for sale would be violating the terms of his or her federal license, thereby breaking the law.

For many years now there have been beers incorporating hempseed or other non-intoxicating hemp derivatives that are produced by professional brewers and federally approved for sale. This is because the seeds of the cannabis variety that produces hemp do not contain psychoactive THC, or at least not at a level considered worrisome by regulatory authorities. Remember that old song, "Down to Seeds and Stems Again Blues"? No? Well, never mind, I'm sure you get the idea.

Like hops, the flower in cannabis is where the essence of the herbal experience lies. The two plants, as you've probably heard, are also botanical cousins, with a lot of similarities. While cannabis plants are reproduced and cultivated only by seed, hops are re-cultivated almost exclusively by the separation and replanting of rhizomes (although hop plants can also be reproduced by seed). This ensures the nearly universal agricultural occurrence of female hop plants, which is the only one worth much of anything for the purposes for which hops have been identified (the same can be said for cannabis). With hops, since rhizomes are an option for reproduction (they don't occur in cannabis), keeping males out of the picture devotes the nutritive attentions of the female plants to the production of beautiful, resinous flowers rather than useless seeds. Female cannabis plants are built to produce seeds, but they are also built to produce the precursors of THC in their flowers, a concentration of effort also encouraged by the trimming of extraneous growth. The male cannabis plants? I'm not sure what they do, but they don't flower nearly as convincingly as the females; the less said about their ambitions the better. The leaves of both female and male cannabis plants contain THC too, but it is in the flowers of cannabis and hops where pure girl power is embodied, and, according to tastes and inclinations, that's what we like.

Now, I'll be honest. I have drunk beers made with hempseed only grudgingly myself, and never with any particular enjoyment. The sheer, well, seediness is a flavor that just doesn't appeal to me. If hempseed tasted like cumin or grains of paradise it might be a different story, but it strikes me that the whole reason they've ever been produced is as a nudge in the ribs, a novelty just this side of legal. CBD beers claim some therapeutic or otherwise nominally noticeable effect, but flavor-wise?—I'm not so sure. But the flowers, that's altogether different. The flowers are imbued with terpenic intensity. Connoisseurs, of course, are able to differentiate between different pot varieties and their consequent effect (not just when smoked, but when used in brewing beer) the way the rest of us do when rubbing, sniffing, and otherwise evaluating hops. If you read through the sensory descriptions used for brief evaluation of particular hop varieties, you'll occasionally encounter mention of cannabis. And once you get to thinking about it, hop intensity in IPA almost invites the introduction of weed intensity, should a brewer—a homebrewer—be so inclined. Therefore, we should probably take a look at it. Cannabis, in case you're taxonomically curious, is definitely an herb.

Now for some basic facts. If all you're looking for by introducing cannabis to your beer is an herbal touch of flavor or aroma, you can probably get that by using it as you might any other herb, that is, steeping it on the hot side of the brewing process, or adding it to fermentation or conditioning on the cold side. These methods will not, however, imbue the beer with THC, as this compound needs to be unlocked by heating and solubilizing in some type of alcohol or fat (and no, the amount of alcohol in conventional beer isn't enough). One of these two methods will work: crafting a tincture in some kind of high-proof and relatively flavorless liquor or spirit like rum, vodka, or Everclear; or by making an infusion of butter, olive oil, or some other fatty substance. In both cases the application of heat is also required, which speeds up the decarboxylation of THCA (tetrahydrocannabinolic acid, a precursor of THC) into THC (simple air drying also does this, but less effectively). This must be done initially by the application of dry heat and then, ideally, whether using the alcohol or fat method, by infusion in a jar or similar container followed by prolonged immersion in a water bath of constant temperature, such as that used in sous vide cooking.

Butter in beer doesn't sound fabulous, for many reasons, but other oils such as olive, coconut, or avocado are far less potentially unpleasant. Olive oil, in fact, whether infused or not, has been documented as a yeast-beneficial substance that can go a long way toward eliminating the need for post-brew, pre-fermentation wort oxygenation (Hull 2008). For homebrewers, for whom this oxygenating step in the brewing process has long been a procedural bugaboo, simply mixing an olive oil infusion with yeast slurry prior to pitching might seem an attractive option. Not only that, but there's also evidence to suggest that introducing olive oil in this way won't negatively affect the head retention of the resultant beer, something which has long plagued many cocoa and coconut beers. However, I should point out that the amount of infused olive oil it is appropriate to use in this process may be insufficient to impart much in the way of psychoactivity in the finished beer; hence the olive oil method may be more conceptual than practical.

In the Recipe section of this chapter I include a recipe employing the alcohol method, gratefully acknowledging the help of Ryan Thomas of Hop Barley and the Alers homebrewing club; but thanks also to Ross Koenigs of New Belgium for discussion of the oil method. As it happens, both Ryan and Ross live in Colorado, one of the pioneering states (along with my own home state of Washington) for legalization of recreational cannabis. And no, in case you're wondering, New Belgium itself has not produced THC-infused beer.

SPICES, PEPPERCORNS, AND CHILIES

Where herbs can be fairly reliably defined as the leaves and flowers of the plants with which they are associated, spices by contrast are all over the map. Variously bark, nut, berry, root, pod, seed, nib, husk, grain, or peel, spices are also wildly different in their flavors and effects, and generally more bold than herbs. Differences can also occur from part to part within a single plant. It's reasonably well known that cilantro and coriander come from the same plant, constituting its leaves and seeds, respectively (English speakers outside North America refer to "fresh coriander" or "coriander leaves" rather than the Spanish *cilantro*); similarly, the stalks of celery, its seeds, and its root provide very different culinary effects. Somewhat more obscurely, the spice known as mace comes from the pods in which nutmeg grows. Cinnamon and cassia are more difficult to tease apart, and seem mainly to differ by place of origin more than anything else. Few of these, it might as well be observed, would seem to jump out at the prospective crafter of IPA, but spices should not be categorically written off simply out of confusion, especially when combinations and subtle use are considered. There's a world of difference, and nuance, to be explored when considering them for use in brewing IPA.

Spices are less commonly evoked than herbs in the descriptors employed for hop flavors and aromas (though some of the so-called noble hops are exceptions to this), but have a lot of (selective) possibility for jazzing up IPA. Seeds figure prominently in the roster of spices that seem to correspond most appropriately with flavors in beer: anise, cumin, dill, fenugreek, mustard, poppy, and grains of paradise, for example. Many of these also respond well to roasting, and can develop distinctive flavors and aromas possibly tying in more comprehensively with esters and malt. Fenugreek, for example, develops a maple note when roasted and is, in fact, a constituent ingredient in artificial maple syrup; cumin too becomes something altogether different when tossed in a hot pan or roasted in the oven.

Largely because of their variety, peppercorns deserve special mention, and judiciously used can contribute an array of flavor (and otherwise sensory) notes to IPA. Green, black, and white peppercorns, of course, are different guises of a single organism (immature, mature, and husked, respectively), whereas pink peppercorns are of a different plant altogether and offer a distinctive and very different effect. More so than other peppercorns, Sichuan pepper responds well to roasting; do not, however, attempt this if all you can get is the ground product (the Geneva Convention, I believe, has rules governing procedures like this). Sichuan pepper carries a cultural connotation as well and, like some of the constituent spices of curry, could be combined for harmonic and conceptual effect.

The fact that so many different kinds of chilies in so many different forms are available alongside spices in the aisles and catalogs of specialty merchants makes it at least expedient to include these vegetables in our consideration of spicing IPA. For chili peppers such as cayenne, ancho, and the various New Mexico varieties, roasting, drying, and milling renders their form, use, and effect into something more like spicing than anything else. The earthiness and sweetness of milder types and the heat of the fiercer ones offer an array of both flavor and sensation that, if such things are to your taste (and that of your customers), can combine in interesting ways with the sweet, bitter, and otherwise aromatic qualities of an IPA thoughtfully conceived and executed to incorporate them. The general notion of chilies in beer has both its adherents and its detractors, having mostly to do with (in my opinion) the fact that many examples of chili beers in the past have been turned with a pretty heavy hand. Like hop bitterness imparted to extremes, over-Scovillization of both food and beer is a phenomenon frequently linkable to dubious machismo. More subtly manipulated and introduced in artful combination, chilies in IPA can be a delicious, even indefinable, element. Once again, it's all about balance. Like peppercorns in all their chromatic variation, chilies can provide both flavor and heat.

It's Clobberin' Time!

I've alluded here and there to the grinding of spices, chilies, and herbs to enhance their efficacy, and perhaps a few more words on the subject are warranted. Like coffee, freshly ground is best, whenever possible, and many purveyors will grind things freshly for you. On a large scale, perhaps, one might choose to trust the packaging methods of a reputable merchant to keep from having to grind or mill vast quantities of such things on arrival. Just the same, in such situations you might want to consider using a dedicated hammer mill, though it's a good idea to be mindful of resins and oils, which can literally gum up the works. One advantage of such treatment is that the resulting powders can be directly added, unbagged, at stages like the whirlpool without fear of clogging heat exchanging hardware. This is especially effective for dried herbs and flowers.

As with all other ingredients, freshness is a watchword where herbs, spices, flowers, shoots, and the like are concerned. We should probably all clear out our cupboards, given the inevitable age of the herbs and spices therein, and restock them with new stuff. As with making beer itself, supplies should be closely tailored to usage in order to make sure that what we cook and brew with, and drink, are the best and most effective they can be.

As with many of the other ingredients we discuss in connection with augmentation of IPA, the subject of herbs and spices sprawls across classifications and practical uses. Once again, the charts later in this chapter will offer a more complete presentation and analysis (tables 4.1 and 4.2).

IPA RECIPES WITH HERBS AND SPICES

Avatar Jasmine IPA (For 5 US gallons [19 L])

Jasmine IPA

Original gravity: 1.066 (16.5°P)
Final gravity: 1.019 (4.75°P)
Color: 5.5 SRM
Bitterness: 50 IBU
ABV: 6.8%

GRAIN BILL
92% 11 lb. (5 kg) Great Western Malting Northwest Select 2-row malt
4% 8 oz. (225 g) Weyermann Munich malt
2% 4 oz. (112 g) Weyermann Carahell malt
2% 4 oz. (112 g) Crisp 45°L crystal malt

HOPS
1.75 oz. (50 g) Northern Brewer (8.5% AA) @ 90 min.
1.5 oz. (42 g) Glacier (5.6% AA) @ 2 min.
1.5 oz. (42 g) Amarillo (9.2% AA) @ whirlpool

ADDITIONAL INGREDIENTS
1.5 oz. (42 g) dried jasmine flowers (bagged) @ 10 min.
0.5 oz. (14 g) dried jasmine flowers (bagged) @ whirlpool

YEAST
Imperial Yeast A07 Flagship

BREWING NOTES
Mash 60 min. @ 153°F (67°C).
Boil 90 min., adding jasmine at appropriate times.
Ferment until terminal, then transfer to secondary.
Condition @ 35°F (2°C) 1 week until bright
Carbonate to 2.5 volumes (4.9 g/L) CO_2.

Green Dragon IPA *(For 5 US gallons [19 L])*

Marijuana IPA

Thanks to Ryan Thomas of Hop Barley and the Alers homebrewing club in Colorado.

Original gravity: 1.059 (15.7°P)
Final gravity: 1.008 (2°P)
Color: 4.9 SRM
Bitterness: 100+ IBU
ABV: 6.7%

GRAIN BILL
94% 12 lb. (5.5 kg) Golden Promise™ pale malt
4% 8 oz. (225 g) Vienna malt
2% 4 oz. (112 g) 40°L crystal malt

TINCTURE
(For 20 U.S. gallons [76 L] beer)
0.125 oz. (3.5 g) cannabis flowers of choice—suggestion is for Sour Diesel or
    Blue Dream
2 oz. (56 g) liquor rated 151 proof (75.5% ABV) or more, e.g., Everclear or
    overproof rum

To make tincture:

Preheat oven to 325°F (170°C).

Finely grind cannabis and spread on a sheet of aluminum foil.

Bake for 5 min., during time it will darken to brownish green.

Remove from oven and blend with liquor in small mason jar.

Sous vide (or simmer in water) the sealed mason jar at 170°F (77°C)—just below the boiling point for alcohol—for 20 min.

Strain mixture and press to extract all liquid—you will get about 1 fl. oz. (30 mL).

CAUTION: USE ONLY ONE-QUARTER OF THIS AMOUNT FOR 5 GAL. (19 L) OF BEER. The above instructions are to make production manageable. THIS IS ENOUGH TOTAL TINCTURE FOR 20 GAL. (76 L) OF BEER.

HOPS

0.25 oz. (7 g) blend of Galaxy, Simcoe, and Mosaic @ mash

0.75 oz. (21 g) blend of Galaxy, Simcoe, and Mosaic @ wort recirculation

3 oz. (85 g) blend of Galaxy, Simcoe, and Mosaic @ first wort

4 oz. (112 g) blend of Galaxy, Simcoe, and Mosaic @ whirlpool

4 oz. (112 g) blend of Galaxy, Simcoe, and Mosaic @ dry hop

WATER

43 ppm calcium, 36 ppm sodium, 140 ppm sulfate, 56 ppm chloride, 2 mg magnesium

YEAST

Wyeast 1056

BREWING NOTES

Mash 60 min. @ 152°F (67°C).

Boil 90 min.

Ferment until terminal, then transfer to secondary.

Condition @ 35°F (2°C) 1 week until bright.

Add 0.25 fl. oz. (7–8 mL) tincture before packaging/kegging; mix well.

Carbonate to 2.5 volumes (4.9 g/L) CO_2.

Pods and Sods IPA *(For 5 US gallons [19 L])*

Tamarind Kaffir Lime IPA

Original gravity: 1.062 (15.5°P)
Final gravity: 1.017 (4.25°P)
Color: 6.71 SRM (without fruit)
Bitterness: 58 IBU
ABV: 5.9%

GRAIN BILL
93% 10.5 lb. (4.8 kg) American 2-row malt
<2.5% 4 oz. (112 g) Weyermann Munich malt
<2.5% 4 oz. (112 g) Weyermann Carahell malt
<2.5% 4 oz. (112 g) Crisp 30°L crystal malt

HOPS
7.5 oz. (213g) Waimea (17.5% AA) @ 90 min.
1.0 oz. (28 g) Waimea (17.5% AA) @ 10 min.
2.0 oz. (56 g) Hallertau Blanc (10.5% AA) @ 2 min.
0.5 oz. (14 g) Hallertau Blanc (10.5% AA) @ whirlpool

ADDITIONAL INGREDIENTS
1 oz. (28 g) kaffir lime leaf (bruised) @ whirlpool
6 fl. oz. (180 mL) tamarind concentrate

YEAST
Wyeast 1056

BREWING NOTES
Mash 60 min. @ 153°F (67°C).
Boil 90 min.
Add bruised kaffir lime leaves in whirlpool.
Add tamarind concentrate to fermentor.
Ferment until terminal, then transfer to secondary.
Condition @ 35°F (2°C) 1 week until bright.
Carbonate to 2.5 volumes (4.9 g/L) CO_2.

ADDITIONAL NOTES

Tamarind is sold as whole pods, in a block like old-fashioned chewing tobacco, or as concentrate in liquid form. The first two involve processing and straining, the third does not.

June of '66 IPA *(For 5 US gallons [19 L])*

Rosemary IPA

Original gravity: 1.066 (16.5°P)
Final gravity: 1.012 (3°P)
Color: 6.28 SRM
Bitterness: 61 IBU
ABV: 6.8%

GRAIN BILL

90% 12 lb. (5.5 kg) Rahr 2-row malt
4% 8 oz. (225 g) Weyermann Munich malt
2% 4 oz. (112 g) Weyermann CaraVienne malt
2% 4 oz. (112 g) Crisp 45°L crystal malt
>1% 3 oz. (85 g) Weyermann Carared® malt
<1% 2 oz. (56 g) Weyermann Carahell malt

HOPS

2.25 oz. (64 g) Chinook (13% AA) @ 90 min.
1.5 oz. (42 g) Dr. Rudi (11% AA) @ 10 min.
1.5 oz. (42 g) Dr. Rudi (11% AA) @ 2 min.
1 oz. (28 g) Dr. Rudi (11% AA) @ whirlpool

ADDITIONAL INGREDIENTS

2 oz. (56 g) rosemary branches, cut into 2" pieces @ mash
1 oz. (28 g) rosemary needles @ whirlpool
1 oz. (28 g) rosemary needles @ conditioning

YEAST

Imperial Yeast A07 Flagship

BREWING NOTES

Mash 60 min. @ 153°F (67°C) with rosemary branches.

Boil 90 min.

Add second rosemary addition to whirlpool.

Ferment until terminal, then transfer to secondary.

Condition @ 35°F (2°C) 1 week until bright, with more rosemary needles (bagged).

Carbonate to 2.5 volumes (4.9 g/L) CO_2.

Shiso Fine IPA *(For 5 US gallons [19 L])*

Shiso Pink Peppercorn IPA

Thanks to Kim Jordan of New Belgium Brewing.

Original gravity: 1.060 (15°P)
Final gravity: 1.017 (4.25°P)
Color: 5.36 SRM
Bitterness: 73 IBU
ABV: 5.7%

GRAIN BILL

92% 11 lb. (5 kg) American 2-row malt

4% 8 oz. (225 g) Carapils® malt

4% 8 oz. (225 g) 30°L crystal malt

HOPS

1.25 oz. (35 g) Waimea (17.5% AA) @ 90 min.

1.5 oz. (42 g) Waimea (17.5% AA) @ 5 min.

1.5 oz. (42 g) German Northern Brewer (8.5% AA) @ 5 min.

0.5 oz. (14 g) German Northern Brewer (8.5% AA) @ whirlpool

ADDITIONAL INGREDIENTS

1 cup (~30–40 g) semi-tightly packed shiso leaves, ribboned

2 oz. (56 g) crushed pink peppercorns

YEAST

Imperial Yeast A07 Flagship

BREWING NOTES

Mash 60 min. @ 153°F (67°C).

Boil 90 min.

Ferment until terminal, then transfer to secondary with shiso and pink peppercorns.

Condition @ 35°F (2°C) 1 week until bright.

Carbonate to 2.5 volumes (4.9 g/L) CO_2.

The Cs Knees IPA *(For 5 US gallons [19 L])*

Gin Botanical IPA

Thanks to Jason Parker of Copperworks Distilling, Seattle, Washington for help with proportions of botanicals.

Original gravity: 1.065 (16.25°P)
Final gravity: 1.010 (2.5°P)
Color: 9 SRM
Bitterness: 61 IBU
ABV: 7.2%

GRAIN BILL

92% 12 lb. (5.5 kg) Thomas Fawcett Maris Otter malt

3% 6 oz. (170 g) Weyermann Munich malt

3% 6 oz. (170 g) Crisp caramalt

2% 4 oz. (112 g) Crisp 45°L crystal malt

HOPS

1.75 oz. (50 g) Chinook (13% AA) @ 90 min.

0.5 oz. (14 g) Centennial (10% AA) @ 5 min.

0.5 oz. (14 g) Cascade (5.5% AA) @ 5 min.

0.5 oz. (14 g) Centennial (10% AA) @ 2 min.

0.5 oz. (14 g) Cascade (5.5% AA) @ 2 min.

0.5 oz. (14 g) Citra (12% AA) @ whirlpool

ADDITIONAL INGREDIENTS
1 oz. (28 g) lemon zest @ whirlpool
0.5 oz. (14 g) dried Seville orange peel @ whirlpool
0.5 oz. (14 g) crushed juniper berries @ whirlpool
0.25 oz. (7 g) crushed cubeb berries @ whirlpool
0.25 oz. (7 g) orris root @ whirlpool
0.25 oz. (7 g) angelica root @ whirlpool

YEAST
Fuller's Yeast

BREWING NOTES
Mash 60 min. @ 151°F (66°C).
Boil 90 min.
Add botanicals to whirlpool.
Ferment until terminal, then transfer to secondary.
Condition @ 35°F (2°C) 1 week until bright.
Carbonate to 2.5 volumes (4.9 g/L) CO_2.

Thyme Has Come Today IPA *(For 5 US gallons [19 L])*

Fresh Thyme IPA

Original gravity: 1.062 (15.5°P)
Final gravity: 1.010 (2.5°P)
Color: 6.29 SRM
Bitterness: 57 IBU
ABV: 6.8%

GRAIN BILL
92% 11 lb. (5 kg) American 2-row malt
4% 8 oz. (225 g) Weyermann Munich malt
2% 4 oz. (112 g) Weyermann Carahell malt
2% 4 oz. (112 g) Crisp 77°L crystal malt

HOPS

1.5 oz. (43 g) Pacific Jade (13% AA) @ 90 min.
0.5 oz. (14 g) Pacific Jade (13% AA) @ 5 min.
0.5 oz. (14 g) Hallertau Blanc (10.5% AA) @ 5 min.
1.5 oz. (42 g) Hallertau Blanc (10.5% AA) @ 2 min.
0.5 oz. (14 g) Hallertau Blanc (10.5% AA) @ whirlpool

ADDITIONAL INGREDIENTS

20–25 sprigs fresh thyme @ whirlpool
Additional thyme for conditioning

YEAST

Wyeast 1056

BREWING NOTES

Mash 60 min. @ 153°F (67°C).
Boil 90 min.
Add thyme to whirlpool, either tied or bagged, remove before KO.
Ferment until terminal, then transfer to secondary.
Add more thyme, bagged if necessary, to conditioning.
Condition @ 35°F (2°C) 1 week until bright.
Carbonate to 2.5 volumes (4.9 g/L) CO_2.

ADDITIONAL NOTES

I like thyme quite a bit by itself, but it combines endlessly with other herbs and a lot of fruits.

TABLE 4.1 LIST OF HERBS AND BOTANICALS AND THEIR ATTRIBUTES FOR USE IN BREWING IPAs

Herb	Form(s)	Attributes	Combinations	Additions	Issues/Comments
Alfalfa	Fresh, dried	Grassy; fermentable when green	Fruit, malt	Mash as fermentable when fresh; grassy aromatic when dried	Quirky, perishable, a conceptual statement
Aloe vera	Pureed, gelatinized	Bitter	In balance with hops	Fermentation	Used in Italian amaro
Basil	Fresh, dried	Minty, sweet, perfumy, herbal	Citrus, stone fruit; mildly cooperative with hop aromas; chilies	Bagged and steeped on cold side; conditioning	Should be a good lurker behind malt sturdiness and hop aroma; steep in hot water to experiement
Bay laurel	Dried leaves	Musty-herbal	Citrus, chili, thyme	Whirlpool to soften and volatilize; cold conditioning	A leafy-herbal note, should not dominate
Bayberry	Crushed berries	Fruity-floral	Flowers	Late boil or whirlpool for infusion	Waxy and floral-smelling
Birch	Sap or syrup	Lightly minty	Berries, apples	Fermentation, cold conditioning	An intriguing touch—minty without being mint
Blackberry leaf	Dried, tea	Fragrant, fruity, sweet	Citrus, stone fruit, flowers, hops	Late boil or whirlpool for infusion	Heady and aromatic
Bog myrtle (sweetgale)	Dried	Musty, bitter	Other bitter herbs; yeast phenols	Late boil or whirlpool for infusion	Traditional in gruit as bittering agent
Borage	Fresh or dried flowers	Cucumber	Citrus, pineapple, cucumber	Whirlpool or cold infusion	Mild cucumber aroma
Burdock root	Fresh or dried	Carrot, turnipy	Aromatic herbs, shiso	Mash; infusion added to conditioning	Quieter than carrot, less cabbagey than other root vegetables
Calendula	Dried flowers	Chamomile-like, quiet	Tropical fruit, tea	Late boil or whirlpool for infusion	Mustily herbal, buttery
Chamomile	Dried leaves	full-flavored and marigold-like, buttery	Lavender, other tea herbs, lemon, orange	Late boil or whirlpool for infusion	Somewhat polarizing, not for everyone

Table 4.1 continued on next page

TABLE 4.1 (cont.)

Herb	Form(s)	Attributes	Combinations	Additions	Issues/Comments
Chapparal leaf	Dried leaves	Musty, resinous, and pungent; mildly sage-like	Stone fruit, cactus, kiwi	Late boil or whirlpool for infusion	Evocative of the desert
Chervil	Fresh or dried leaves	Sharp, creosote, oregano-like	Basil (to mitigate sweetness), thyme	Late boil or whirlpool for infusion	Best in combination rather than alone
Chives	Fresh or dried	Mildly oniony and green	Some hops as an accent	Cold conditioning (hot side too strong)	Use carefully; also could be French press-infused with finished beer
Cilantro (coriander leaf)	Fresh or dried leaves	Sharp and soapy	Citrus peel, curry spices, sweet herbs	Cold infusion	A sharply herbal addition—nervy
Curry leaf	Fresh leaves	Citrus-like, anise, lemongrass	Citrus, ginger, cardamom, turmeric	Whirlpool or cold infusion	Bruise and perhaps dry-fry leaves before using; an intriguing savory flavor
Dill	Fresh or dried	Musty-herbal	Cucumber, lemon, peach, mango	Cold conditioning	Very distinctive and tradition-bound—try something new to combine with it
Echinacea	Dried flowers	Floral, bitter	Lemon, elderberry, mint	Whirlpool	Strong flavor best used in combination
Elderflower	Dried flowers	Floral, a haunting aroma of honey	Berries, but a good stand-alone	Whirlpool	St. Germain, need I say more? But great in beer
Epazote	Fresh or dried	Resinous, mildly sharp	Squash, lime, chili	Whirlpool or cold infusion	Dried easier to get, but fresh more lively
Fennel	Chopped or pureed bulbs; fresh fronds; whole or ground seeds; flowers	Licorice; bulb somewhat celery-like; leaves a cross between anise and dill	Licoricey hops, stone fruits	Fronds in mash or cold side; pureed bulbs in fermentation; flowers and seeds in cold conditioning	Many ways to play it, varying intensities
Garlic chives	Fresh	More garlic aroma than regular chives	Garlic or oniony hops, oregano	Cold conditioning	See Chives

Herb	Form(s)	Attributes	Combinations	Additions	Issues/Comments
Gentian	Dried root	Extremely bitter	Hops, other bitter herbs	Whirlpool or cold infusion	Classic bittering ingredient in amaro, Angostura bitters, Underberg, and other liqueurs; also Moxie
Hawthorn	Berries	Apples, tart	Other berries, rose hip	Whirlpool; cold infusion of crushed berries	Tart and somewhat bitter; in the rose family
Heather	Fresh or dried flowers	Mildly perfumy and evergreen	Malt, flowery hops, mild teas	Mash for a beautiful sparkle and aromatic wort; whirlpool; cold infusion in conditioning	Fragile aroma driven off by heat, most haunting on the cold side
Hibiscus	Dried flowers	Tart, sour	Sour treatments, tropical fruit	Late boil or whirlpool for infusion	Haunting tart addition
Honeysuckle	Fresh or dried flowers	Perfumy and sweet	Citrus, stone fruit; quieter hop aromas	As late as possible—fragile	They'll never smell as good as they do on the bush, but still worth trying
Horehound	Dried flowers	Bitter	Other bitter herbs	Whirlpool or cold infusion	One of Passover's bitter herbs; also once thought to be anti-magical
Hyssop	Fresh leaves	Herbal-anise, camphor, pine	Herb blends	Cold conditioning	An anise-like element to an herbal blend
Jasmine	Dried flowers	Floral, grapey	Floral hops, other flowers	Late boil or whirlpool for infusion	Can vary in intensity from strawlike to grapey
Juniper	Branches	Evergreen perfume, resinous bite	Hops; other gin botanicals, e.g., orris, coriander; flower teas	Branches in brewing liquor or mash (also cold infusion in conditioning); berries late hot side or cold infusion	Cut branches fairly small for mash addition, otherwise beware runoff and mash-out; sterilize and hang whole branches in cold conditioning; beware poisonous varieties
Kaffir lime	Fresh or dried leaves	Savory citrus	Lemongrass, ginger and galangal, coriander	Whirlpool or cold infusion	Nice addition to a concept IPA

Table 4.1 continued on next page

TABLE 4.1 (cont.)

Herb	Form(s)	Attributes	Combinations	Additions	Issues/Comments
Lavender	Fresh or dried flowers	Grandma aroma	Hops, other flowers; citrus peel or fruit	Cold conditioning	Polarizing—lovely to some, soapy to others
Lemon verbena	Fresh or dried leaves	Terpenic and lemony	Fenugreek, caraway, hops, ginger	Late boil, whirlpool, cold infusion	Mild and pleasantly multi-dimensional; native to Argentina
Lemongrass	Chopped stalks	Lemony-tropical—compelling	Tamarind, turmeric, ginger	Whirlpool or cold infusion	Haunting, compelling, a natural
Licorice root	Chopped root	Anise, celery	Continental hops, citrus, stone fruit	Mash, whirlpool, cold infusion	Strong and earthy, could be a nice back note
Lovage	Fresh leaves	Sharp, bold, cilantro-celery	Pepper, resinous hops	Cold infusion	Very bold, try it first in combination with cold food
Maple	Sap or syrup	Mild sweetness (sap); bold, no-doubt-about-it maple (syrup)	Hops, wood aging, nut tannins	Sap as brewing liquor; syrup in fermentation	Requires subdued use to avoid conceptual slavishness
Marjoram	Dried leaves	Resinous, quietly oregano-like	Chives, basil, thyme, mint	Late boil, whirlpool, cold infusion	See Chervil and Oregano
Meadowsweet	Dried leaves and flowers	Tannic, astringent, aromatic	Other flowers, mild herbs	Whirlpool or cold infusion	Also contains salicylic acid (constituent of aspirin)
Mint	Fresh leaves	Well, minty, but many varieties	Citrus; apple and pear	Cold infusion	Not often successful, but I still believe . . .
Myrrh	Resin chunks	Perfumy and resinous, bitter	Floral herbs	Whirlpool—heat needed to dissolve	Strong perfume, could work
Oregano	Fresh or dried	Resinous, especially Mexican	Basil, marjoram	Whirlpool or cold infusion	Resinous note can tie in with hops, but can dominate

Herb	Form(s)	Attributes	Combinations	Additions	Issues/Comments
Orris	Roots, extract	Floral, herbal	Anything else herbal or botanical; also acts as a fixative, a joiner of other elements	Cold conditioning	A flavor binder in addition to its own flavor/aroma
Patchouli	Leaves	Inescapably aromatic	Marijuana, sandalwood	Shouldn't get any closer than the barstool and then only if paying for beer	Almost universally loathed, but it is a natural aroma
Pennyroyal	Fresh or dried leaves	Minty	Pepper, sage	Whirlpool or cold infusion	An often wild mint, used in teas
Pine	New bright green tips	Resinous, evergreen	Hops, flower teas	Cold conditioning	Unmistakable evergreen character
Pineapple sage	Fresh or dried leaves	Pineapple	Citrus, pineapple, other tropical fruits	Whirlpool or cold infusion	Leaves smell like pineapple
Queen Anne's lace	Root	Carroty	Other aromatic roots, caraway	Mash, whirlpool, cold infusion	Nice touch for a foraged beer
Rose	Dried flowers	Roselike	Anything stronger to reduce it to an accent	Whirlpool or cold infusion	Careful, but if you're a rose fan . . .
Rose hip	Chopped fresh	Mildly floral, tart, lemony	Berries, apples (related), pink peppercorns	Cold conditioning	Nice tart addition, mild
Rosemary	Branches or separated needles	Resinous, piney, woodsy	Thyme, sage; smoke, wood	Branches in mash and cold conditioning; bagged needles in whirlpool	Use a lot, especially if it grows easily where you live
Sage	Fresh or dried leaves	Musty, resinous	Citrus, stone fruit, berries, thyme, mints	Whirlpool or cold infusion	Distinctive—a commitment

Table 4.1 continued on next page

TABLE 4.1 (cont.)

Herb	Form(s)	Attributes	Combinations	Additions	Issues/Comments
Sassafras	Whole, broken, or ground leaves	Complex, spicy, rich, camphor-like	Thyme, persimmon, pineapple	Whirlpool or cold infusion	The heart of the flavor of filé gumbo
Schisandra	Berries	Tart, intense, take-charge	Wood treatments; sweet fruits	Mill and add to boil, whirlpool, or fermentor	Claim to fame is that it covers all five flavors
Shiso	Fresh or dried leaves; alcohol infusion	Bold, dominant, pleasantly meaty	Citrus, peach, plum, salt	Cold conditioning, either chopped leaves or an alcohol infusion	Unfamiliar enough to many to be worth a try; bold, satisfying, and unique
Sorrel	Fresh foraged leaves	Peppery, tart, grassy	Tart fruits, pawpaw, papaya	Mash (if quantities permit); cold infusion	Grassy and sharp, could provide good counterpoint
Spruce	New bright green tips	Sweetly evergreen, mild cola flavor	Honey, agave, hops, ginger	Cold infusion, including in keg	More than just pitch flavored; complex and spicy-fruity
Sweet cicely (Myrrhis odorata)	Fresh leaves	Anise, carrot	Herb blends	Cold conditioning	Often used in aquavit; used in blends
Sweet grass (bison grass)	Fresh or dried	Cinnamon	Ginger, peach	Whirlpool or cold infusion	Also called bison grass, similar to woodruff
Sweet woodruff	Fresh or dried leaves	Vanilla, mild cinnamon or allspice	Malt, grassy hops	Cold infusion	Very mild, more grassy character when fresh; comes into its own when dried
Tarragon	Fresh or dried leaves	Savory, distinctive	Carrots, parsnips	Cold infusion	Twice as strong when dried
Thyme	Fresh or dried	Minty, resinous, aromatic	Berries, stone fruit	Late boil, whirlpool, cold infusion	A must-use herb for IPA, works hand in glove with hops
Tobacco	Whole fermented leaves	Full, rich, scary	Stone fruit, persimmon, basil, thyme	Cold infusion	Certainly not approved for commercial use, but a hearty, alarmingly rich depth of flavor

Herb	Form(s)	Attributes	Combinations	Additions	Issues/Comments
Vietnamese coriander	Fresh or dried leaves	Soapy, sharp	Citrus peel, curry spices, sweet herbs	Cold infusion	Similar to regular coriander, but flourishes in heat
Violet	Dried or candied flowers	Floral, haunting, identifiable	Citrus, stone fruit	Whirlpool or cold infusion	A statement, but could combine very nicely
Wormwood	Dried leaves	Anise, menthol effect	Other anise herbs for combination with anise-flavored hops	Cold conditioning	Also anti-microbial; good for an absinthe-concept IPA
Walnut	Outer husks	Tannic, a splash of brown color	Sage, thyme, ginger; wood treatments	Cold infusion	A puckery touch—easy there
Yarrow	Dried leaves/needles	Minty, pleasant, mildly rosemary-like	Other gruit herbs	Cold infusion	Traditional bittering herb

TABLE 4.2 LIST OF SPICES AND THEIR ATTRIBUTES FOR USE IN BREWING IPAs

Spice	Form(s)	Attributes	Combinations	Additions	Issues/Comments
Allspice	Seeds crushed or ground	Sweet and clove-like	Sassafras, aromatic hops	Whirlpool, cold conditioning	Strong, fruit aroma and flavor, should be used sparingly in IPA
Angelica	Roots and seeds	Carroty, dill-like	Other bitter herbs	Cold conditioning	A common gin botanical, related to carrot and Queen Anne's lace
Anise (aniseed)	Seeds whole or ground	Licorice	Some medium-alpha Continental hops	Whirlpool, cold conditioning	A complement to hops and other bitter herbs
Annatto	Seeds whole or ground	Earthy, slightly peppery	Probably only a back note	Whirlpool	Mainly used as a coloring (poor man's saffron)
Asafoetida	Leaves; powdered (more likely)	Compelling sour-oniony taste	Indian spices	Whirlpool	Interesting, indefinable flavor; acts as a flavor enhancer
Caraway	Whole or ground	Rye bread/aquavit, carroty, grassy and sharp	Pepper, dill, cilantro, coriander	Whirlpool, cold conditioning	Strong flavor, works well in herbal combination—take courage!
Cardamom	Whole pods or ground	Musty and strongly-flavored, but interesting alone or with other spices	Other Indian or Mexican spices, stone fruits	Whirlpool, cold conditioning	Could provide a nice, indefinable accent
Cardamom, black	Pods crushed or ground	Smoky (since heat-cured), gingery-spicy	Slovenian hops, coriander	Whirlpool, cold conditioning	Interesting smoky spice—gotta be a place for it
Cardamom, green	Pods crushed or ground	Gingery-spicy	Other Indian spices, Continental hops	Whirlpool, cold conditioning	A spicy sharpness quieter than many others
Cascarilla	Bark pieces whole or ground	Bitter, compelling	Bittering hops, thyme, tobacco	Whirlpool, cold conditioning	Used in bitter aperitifs; once used as an additive to cigarettes

Spice	Form(s)	Attributes	Combinations	Additions	Issues/Comments
Cinnamon	Crushed sticks or ground	Dominant, recognizable	Apple or pear; other curry spices	Boil, whirlpool, cold conditioning	A bold statement, test before committing
Cassia (Chinese cinnamon)	Whole sticks crushed or ground	Less ethereal, more work-manlike than cinnamon	Same as cinnamon, but choose for yourself	Whirlpool, cold conditioning	Double roll, thicker bark than "true" cinnamon; typically used in bolder, more savory dishes than cinnamon
Cinnamon	Whole sticks crushed or ground	Spicy, sharp, and satisfying	Malt touches, wood aging	Whirlpool, cold conditioning	Typically used in sweeter dishes than cassia; many origins, Vietnamese the hottest—easy there
Cloves	Whole or ground	Heady, strong spiciness	The effect is akin to charred wood	Whirlpool, cold conditioning	Could theoretically work with the precisely right hop combination, but I'm skeptical
Coriander	Seeds whole or ground	Perfumy	Citrus peel, curry spices, sweet herbs	Late boil or whirl-pool, cold infusion	Traditional in other styles; its use in IPA would be offbeat
Cubeb berries	Crushed or ground	Peppery, resinous, with a tang	Other gin botanicals, other peppercorns	Whirlpool, cold conditioning	An unusual pepperiness
Cumin	Whole seed or ground	Smoky, warm, spicy-sweet	Other Indian or Mexican spices, stone fruits	Whirlpool, cold conditioning	Also try dry roasting whole seeds before grinding
Dill seed	Whole seed or ground	Sharp, vegetal	Cucumber lemon; Sorachi Ace hops	Whirlpool, cold conditioning	Easy does it; could tie in with certain hop varieties
Fennel seed	Whole seed or ground	Licorice, milder than anise	Coriander; Continental hops	Whirlpool, cold conditioning	A quieter, approachable licorice flavor
Fenugreek	Ground seeds	Maple-like, especially when roasted	Squash, evergreen tips	Whirlpool, cold conditioning	Used in manufacture of artificial maple syrup
Galangal	Peeled and chopped	Very sharp, woody to use	Thai spices, root vegetables, pumpkin	Fermentation	Very hot when concentrated by juicing

Table 4.2 continued on next page

TABLE 4.2 (cont.)

Spice	Form(s)	Attributes	Combinations	Additions	Issues/Comments
Ginger	Peeled and chopped, powdered, or juiced	Hot and tingly	Squash, carrot, stone fruit	Juice for brightest flavor on cold side; more solid, less aromatic touches in whirlpool or fermentation	Odd choice for IPA, but could combine with distinctive and sharp hop flavors/aromas
Grains of paradise	Ground seeds	Jasmine, citrus, ginger, pepper	Other pepper, practically any fruit	Whirlpool, cold conditioning	A nice addition to many beers; very difficult to crush or mill
Horseradish	Fresh, grated root	Sharp and peppery-aromatic	Bold hops, chamomile	Cold conditioning—mash or other hot addition might beat down sharpness	A knife's edge kind of thing—could prove interesting in IPA
Juniper berries	Crushed or powdered	Piney, resinous, aromatic	Piney hops, myrrh, anise, cubeb, other gin additives	Whirlpool, cold conditioning	Easy to use and evaluate, a natural addition to IPA
Long pepper	Whole, crushed, or ground	Hot, fruity	Other peppers, allspice, cumin	Cold conditioning	Recently discovered for beer, fruity heat somewhat unique
Mace	Ground husks	Husk of nutmeg, so similar, but a bit different	Nutmeg (for complexity), other spice, flowers	Whirlpool, cold conditioning	Doesn't scream IPA to me, but could be a back note
Mustard	Whole or ground	Pungent, hearty (different colored seeds)	Cumin, caraway	Cold conditioning	Out there, but some type of mustard could be intriguing
Nigella seed	Whole or ground	Nutty, oniony	Savory food, mainly, but perhaps other pepper or spice	Whirlpool, cold conditioning	Could have interplay with hops as a very quiet touch
Nutmeg	Grated or ground	Aromatic, quintessentially spicy and warm	Some other style, in all likelihood (see mace)	Whirlpool, cold conditioning	Might combine with hop and herb terpenes

Spice	Form(s)	Attributes	Combinations	Additions	Issues/Comments
Pepper, Sichuan	Crushed or ground	Hot, with bonus numbing effect	Stone fruit, apples, tropical fruits	Cold infusion	An effect as much as a flavor; could work well with other sweet effects
Peppercorn, black	Whole or ground	Well, peppery	Citrus, other fruit, other pepper varieties	Whirlpool, cold conditioning	Can liven anything up, perhaps even IPA
Peppercorn, green	Whole or ground	Not quite as hot as black, hotter than white	Spicy hops, other peppers in blend	Whirlpool, cold conditioning	The less ripe form of black pepper
Peppercorn, white	Whole or ground	Bright and sparkly, milder than either black or green	Pink peppercorn, cucumber, carrot	Whirlpool, cold conditioning	The gentlest peppercorn—could be worked in for a nice sparkly effect without dominance
Peppercorn, pink	Crushed or ground	Mildly hot, sweetly fragrant and a bit gummy	Long pepper, thyme, white pepper	Whirlpool, cold conditioning	Fragile—the later the addition the greater the effect
Poppy seed	Whole or ground	Oily, musty, bready	Lightly colored malts	Whirlpool, cold conditioning	Interesting; unusual in beer, especially IPA
Saffron	Threads	Indefinable, heady; pinky-orange color	Mild ginger, sour treatment	Cold infusion	Fun; expensive, but lower-grade medicinal stuff more reasonably priced
Star anise	Whole or ground	Sweet anise, strong	Fruit, pepper	Cold infusion	A little goes a long way
Sumac	Powdered	Tart, lemony	Where you might use lemon	Whirlpool, cold conditioning	Easily foraged, and easily differentiated from poisonous non-related namesake; very difficult to infuse, even in alcohol—patience!
Turmeric	Grated, powdered, or juiced	Amazing orange color; mild herbal sharpness	Ginger, citrus, mint, apple	Cold conditioning	Flavor will creep to the corners, nice color addition
Wasabi	Grated, paste, or powdered	Sharp, nose-filling	Ginger	Cold conditioning	Root very expensive; radical move

HIS DARK MATERIALS: COFFEE AND CHOCOLATE IPA

Roughly contemporaneous with the rise of the craft brewing movement, an artisanal quickening has taken place in the realm of coffee and chocolate. And bread, and cheese, and ice cream, and preserves, and a lot of other, more arcane, stuff. This phenomenon, we all know, is indicative of a larger societal movement to rediscover Real Quality Things, a reaction against the consolidation and toxic homogenization that took place during the post-war and Space Race years of just about everything Americans put into their bodies. Budweiser beer, Folger's coffee, Hershey bars, Wonder bread, Velveeta processed cheese food, and mega-dairy ice creams made with propylene glycol—this was to be the nutriment of the American future. And, now that I think of it, there was a brand of chemical weight-gain milkshake called Nutrament. Oh, what do you know? It still exists, and it's owned by Nestlé.

But fortunately for all of us in the United States, that isn't to be our American future. Other countries didn't make all the mistakes of cleansing and synthesis America did during those years, and managed to selectively keep alive top-notch examples of some of the better things in life: beer in Belgium and Germany; coffee in Italy; chocolate in (once again) Belgium, but also in Holland and Switzerland; cheese and bread in France. Back in the States, we are by no means out of the woods in this regard, but at least we can choose to enjoy products in the above categories made with real ingredients and delicious artistry by small and independent producers in our own land. The interesting thing is how well they often go together. Call it an artisanal covalence. Maybe it's the fermentative aspects of beer, bread, and cheese that make them historical best friends; maybe it's the conceptual perversity of taking one's childhood chemical root beer float and doing it one better by plopping a scoop of artisanal, small-dairy ice cream in a craft-brewed oatmeal stout. Maybe it's also simply because we seem to like to hang out together, able to see eye to eye on the fact that what's important is producing honest stuff that also happens to be delicious. And so we collaborate, person to person and business to business, but also product realm to product realm, like chocolate and peanut butter, but in our case with beer.

Sometimes this can be a bit of a stretch, but so was eating the first lobster. As moderns, as improvisers and seekers for the new, we need to be somewhat tolerant of combinations that on the surface might seem antithetical. Like putting something containing a stimulant, coffee, in something else containing what is technically a depressant, beer; like putting something dark, chocolate, in something pale, IPA. But it's the mark of the epicure—and the artisan—to withhold judgement long enough to see if the idea turns out to be delicious.

The first beers to incorporate coffee or chocolate were dark beers, porters and stouts, which simply by their chromatic correspondence seemed to send out a hailing signal to other dark matter. In addition, the things that made these beers dark (roasted malts) and sometimes sweet (intentionally stifled attenuation through alcoholic strength or the addition of non-fermentable sugars) once more suggested correspondence with things dark and roasted, rich and variously sugary. But coffee and chocolate are not simply dark and roasted, they are also bitter, and in different degrees depending on not only such things as cocoa content (in the case of chocolate) or origin sourcing and bean type (in the case of coffee), but also treatment during roasting. So, setting aside for a moment the darkness of the materials we're talking about, there's a lot to be considered when combining coffee or chocolate or both with a beer that happens not only to be pale, but to have other inherent aspects that can work in either harmony or counterpoint. But maybe first we should consider them separately. There'll be time later on to bring them back together.

CIRCADIAN RHYTHM—
THE SYMBIOSIS OF COFFEE AND BEER

I'm sure I'm not the only one who, over either a cup of coffee or a beer, has shared the fantasy with one's friendly local roaster about combining the talents and appeal of our two businesses into a single symbiotic entity. An artisanal coffee roaster and café that begins service at, say, six o'clock in the morning, gradually giving way as the day advances to serving beers also produced on site, staying open in such a hybrid guise until 2:00 a.m. or so when other bars close, leaving a handful of hours to get the place cleaned and ready for the next day's service. Given that the purity of identity doesn't really matter, the place is free to be both café and brewpub during the hours of overlap, with the optional addition of food, of course, making maximal use of a single space. Well, however often it's been done and discussed—and I hasten say that when I opened my own brewpub in Seattle many years ago we decided, in the face of abundant local expertise where coffee was concerned, that we weren't even going to serve espresso—the bigger concept has mainly been reduced to individual beers with coffee incorporated into their crafting.

This too has had its story arc of knowledge and proficiency, as the first craft-brewed coffee beers either simply added brewed coffee to an existing beer or made coffee in the brew kettle for an addition with approximately the same effect; sometimes, too, brewers simply added ground coffee to the boil phase of the brew. Anyone who tried any of these methods knows that the result was less than perfect—cowboy coffee, anyone? In most cases the richness of coffee was driven off to leave only an astringent memory of what were, presumably, perfectly good and artfully roasted beans. And the clogging! Only a fool would not have at least bagged coffee in the kettle, but even so one would hear of nightmarish blockages in the heat exchanger. Even when coffee was added to the fermentor or conditioning tank, the result could very easily be (and often was) coffee grounds settling in the cones and dishes of tanks, which made for an enormous challenge simply getting the beer out of there (this invariably happening after something delicious having been drawn from the sample valve, safely above the zone of difficulty). I can personally recall, even when outward flow from a fermentor was established, things still getting clogged in hoses and pumps.

The next step along the way was the use of whole roasted beans rather than ground coffee in either fermentation or conditioning (or in some cases in the mash). Some still swear by this method, but it strikes me, and others in the coffee industry who know more than I do, that just as incompletely milling grain could result in delicious beer, costs and efficiencies are less than ideal given the amount of material used. Another drawback to this or any other process involving the marrying of materials by contact is that it is reliant on the brewer's ability to sense when things are at the level they should be, and to then move beer off whatever form of coffee is in the tank—all this determined, once again, by how the beer tastes drawn from a likely remote testing point or two. This, of course, throws the wrinkle of subjective extrapolation into the mix, given that all beans, all roasts are different, and so, inevitably, a certain amount of guesswork is involved. It is therefore very easy to either overdo the effect or be wasteful with ingredients, and very difficult to be consistent where subsequent batches are concerned.

The eventual breakthrough for the use of coffee in beer came from a revolution in artisanal coffee: cold brew. Pioneered, in my belief, by Stumptown Coffee in Portland, Oregon, cold brew involves cold-steeping ground coffee overnight and then drawing it off for immediate service as a cold, iced-coffee kind of beverage, or for packaging and subsequent distribution. Stumptown's founder, Duane Sorensen, is well versed (and well befriended) in craft brewing circles. I believe because of this that Sorensen carried over a couple of beer-ish touches into the presentation of cold brew. Among these is the use of stubby, beer-style bottles for packaging, and also the eventual pouring of it with 100% nitrogen on draft. Now, of course, everyone is doing it, and calling it cold brew too, a term I also believe Duane first coined.

The beauty of cold brew is that it can be measured exactly to taste in combination with beer consistently and repeatedly. The gentleness of cold brew treatment also makes it possible to appreciate the flavor and aroma of more delicate beans and roasts and how they can combine with beer. I believe this is what has made it possible to introduce coffee to beers of lighter weight and effect compared with the ponderous dark beers that pioneered coffee beers. While IPA brings its own pronounced character to the arranged marriage, color is an issue, it must be owned, but given that such a thing as black IPA has entered the brewer's lexicon, cold brew has proven a way to introduce coffee to beer styles that carry some color without its heavier aspects running away with the spoon. For more traditional, paler IPAs, whole beans closely monitored might still be the way to go. But by having a pretty precise idea (by test mixing) of what a particular coffee will taste like in any given beer, however pale or mild, brewers can execute beers displaying elements of coffee beyond simple power and roastiness. This could be the fruitiness of perhaps an Ethiopian coffee, or it could be the spiciness of something from Indonesia or Latin America. Cold brew has made it possible for brewers to exercise the subtleties of process well known to the proficient roaster. It's no surprise given its profile as a leading original artisanal brand that Stumptown is very likely the roaster most solicited for collaborations with craft brewers wanting to use coffee. It's common for Stumptown to provide a few different roasts and combinations of beans, based on what the prospective brewer has told them, to audition before a commitment is made for the beer. It is a far cry from the days of simply throwing grounds into the kettle.

TOO MUCH OF THE GOOD STUFF? CHOCOLATE IN IPA

As with coffee, bitterness is an innate element of chocolate. In its sweetest incarnations, such as those recalled from childhood, this quality has been obliterated by the addition of sugar. Even the Toblerone snatched from the Christmas stocking of the underage sophisticate has quite a bit of honey in it. With the artisanal putting-away of childish things, however, chocolate lovers have come to recognize the bitter beauty of bars with a high cocoa content. Some of these are puckeringly bitter, but for intensity of chocolate flavor they truly can't be beat. They often combine well with other flavors: cinnamon and other spices, chilies, caramel, and salt (and salted caramel). Making and cooking with chocolate, too, has found new life with the availability of such things. But to be honest, combining all this with IPA is a bit of a daunting prospect. Already intensely bitter, the IPA of our waking dreams kind of has this already in hand; malty sweet in the background, we've mainly checked that box as well. There is also the challenge with less bitter milk chocolate of introducing further fats and oils, though no less an authority than Mitch Steele, long of Stone Brewing in Escondido, California and the author of *IPA: Brewing Techniques, Recipes and the Evolution of India Pale Ale,* insists that concerns regarding reduced head retention due to the use of chocolate are generally overblown. A general entente of aroma between IPA and chocolate is an intriguing prospect though, so before we give up on the idea perhaps we should at least consider an alliance.

Recognizing there are thresholds in all things, bitterness can be shared. With a great deal of IPA's hop character coming from aromatic late additions, including dry hopping, it's in conceptual accord to have hop bitterness roll over just a bit to allow other bitter flavors a place to sleep, at the same time ensuring hops in general are announced in no uncertain terms. This combination can also allow a depth of chocolate flavor to intrude, even to waft up into aromatic perception, while still leaving hops in charge. Or at least I think it could, for in fact among the few IPAs incorporating chocolate that I have tasted, hops, which really should be driving, have been crowded into the backseat like younger siblings, rendering the result more a pale beer with variegated bitterness than a real IPA. Finding this balance of concept and effect, of course, is the stuff of experimentation.

Once more like coffee, techniques for incorporating chocolate and its elements into beer have evolved over time. In the early days of chocolate beers, pretty much all of them dark, cocoa was added on the hot side of the brewing process. Ordinary cocoa has a great deal of fat, so these beers often lacked much in the way of residual foam, creating the impression of thickness with a prickly touch of carbonation, but none of the body and opulence of a sturdy beer with a good solid head. For a time, de-fatted cocoa fit the bill, lessening the head-killing effect, and this can still be the way to go when a strong chocolate flavor is the main objective. When playing the IPA bitterness game, however, some conditioning time on cocoa nibs might prove to be a more effective way to impart a controllable measure of flavor and bite while not completely obliterating any elements sitting astride the other side of the seesaw. Cocoa nibs, while expensive, are fairly easy to use in this way. A local source is preferable, as always, but they can be gotten by mail order. Their shelf life is also short, so order what you need each time you need it, or be prepared for the appearance of mold. Some of the same logistical challenges as ground coffee exist as well, necessitating perhaps an extended standpipe in order to transfer the beer off its accompanying biomass. Moreover, consider all the above advice appropriate for black IPA. Unless the bitterness, flavor, and aroma are in full cooperation, what you're making, in my view, is a chocolate-flavored hoppy porter—either that or a timidly conceived beer on which too much money was spent.

Cocoa Pete

Pete Slosberg, eponymous originator of Pete's Wicked Ale back in the mid-1980s (and, as it happens, the bearer of another moniker—Cocoa Pete—in a subsequent entrepreneurial life), is a man with opinions about both chocolate and beer, and chocolate and beer together. His dinners combining chocolate-themed cuisine (not all of it dessert) with beer in different styles are an eye-opening experience. In addition, he's presided over tastings combining chocolate and really hoppy beers, many of them IPAs. His view is that the bitterness of dark chocolate is too much for an enjoyable, harmonious taste combination with IPA, and for that matter with many other beers with a noticeable hop component. For eating alongside beer, Slosberg prefers milk chocolate at around 50% cocoa content. This advice alone doesn't get us to chocolate IPA, but it does give one something to think about.

Consider also that chocolate frequently conducts its travels in the company of others. Vanilla, in fact, very often accompanies chocolate in a sort of symbiotic way, most often in milk chocolate, where in combination with lactose it acts as a sort of delivery system for the bitterer effect of chocolate. Chocolate and orange as well are the best of companions. Various regional cuisines—notably Mexican, with its mole—bring fruit, nuts, spices, and chilies into the mix with chocolate, making use of chocolate's bitterness and heaviness of flavor to create unique and endlessly variable accents for the food it adorns and complements. All of this, for our purposes, bears consideration. Would vanilla alone gum up the works in a beer as bitter and distinctively aromatic as IPA? Mayyybe.

As a Valentine's Day 2017 edition of its "Enjoy By" series acknowledging the fleeting and fragile nature of aromatically hoppy IPA, Stone Brewing has produced IPA combining both chocolate and coffee. Enjoy By 02.14.17 Chocolate & Coffee IPA brought all three elements together in a mellow combination that emphasizes chocolate, but at 9.4% ABV and with a dozen hop varieties! A version of the beer, or at least the concept, lives on as Stone Mocha IPA.

FANCY A MUGGA? IPA MADE WITH TEA

It may come as a surprise, but, aside from water, tea is the world's most consumed beverage. Tea is made from the leaves of an evergreen plant of Asian origin that are put through a series of processes, the sequence and degrees of which determine whether it ends up classified as white, yellow, green, oolong, or black. It can also be fermented or smoked for further treatment. While tea in its many guises is most often presented plain, it combines well, and endlessly, with other herbs, flowers, fruits, and spices to yield blends traditional, exotic, and hippiefied. Earl Grey, in case you didn't know, is made from black tea combined with bergamot orange. Tea takes on flavors and odors very readily, to both its benefit and detriment depending on taste, commercial opportunity, and storage. In fact, some flower-derived teas, such as jasmine, are not actually tea at all, but an infusion of that flower. South American yerba maté, also loosely regarded as tea, is made from an altogether different plant as well.

Where brewers are concerned, tea is an Atlantis of opportunity, a realm almost entirely overlooked, but with a variety and facility that can yield some pretty interesting and fanciful stuff (providing you don't go all baroque and Sleepytime® on us). Some restraint is definitely called for when using tea in IPA, but there's absolutely no reason why it can't offer a whole range of interesting and conceptually compelling beers. After all, however you choose to incorporate geography in your origin narrative, IPA's eponymous land is in Asia and among the world's largest producers of tea.

Although perhaps an over-simplification, the color and intensity of tea is developed through oxidation, which amplifies its tannic aspect. In IPA, white tea might provide a lightly herbal note, while black or oolong would certainly show up more boldly. Tea also contains caffeine, so like coffee introduces an extra, experiential element to beer. Beers I've had containing yerba maté (some of them IPAs) have provided a noticeable lift. Keep in mind when using any tea blends in brewing that when you bring in the tea you bring in all its companions—orange, hibiscus, rose hip, ginger, or raspberry leaf. Be advised of what exactly is in whatever blend you've decided to use. The simpler the better as far as I'm concerned. Mull over the elements of a particular tea as you're enjoying a cup of it and ponder which hops might go well with it.

In the chart at the end of this chapter (table 5.1) I have chosen to touch on uses for general types where coffee, chocolate, and tea is concerned, rather than get lost in the many different worlds of these varied and complex foodstuffs.

IPA RECIPES WITH COFFEE AND CHOCOLATE

East of Java Black IPA *(For 5 US gallons [19 L])*

Black Coffee IPA

Thanks to Duane Sorenson and Nate Armbrust, both of Stumptown Coffee, but also of Puff Coffee and Riff Coffee, respectively, for discussion about coffee in beer.

Original gravity: 1.065 (16.25°P)
Final gravity: 1.018 (4.75°P)
Color: 21.35 SRM
Bitterness: 53 IBU
ABV: 6%

MALTS
88% 10 lb. (4.5 kg) Thomas Fawcett Maris Otter
4.5% 8 oz. (225 g) Weyermann Munich malt
4.5% 8 oz. (225 g) Crisp 70°L crystal malt
1% 2 oz. (56 g) Weyermann Carafa II malt
1% 2 oz. (56 g) Briess Midnight Wheat malt
1% 2 oz. (56 g) Crisp roasted barley malt

HOPS

1.5 oz. (42 g) Chinook (13% AA) @ 90 min.
1.5 oz. (42 g) Centennial (10% AA) @ 5 min.
1.5 oz. (42 g) Cascade (5.5% AA) @ 5 min.
0.5 oz. (14 g) Cascade (5.5% AA) @ whirlpool
0.5 oz. (14 g) Centennial (10% AA) @ whirlpool

ADDITIONAL INGREDIENTS

1 qt. (0.95 L) cold-brewed coffee (made with 4 oz. [112 g] ground top-quality
    artisanally roasted coffee)

YEAST

Imperial Yeast A07 Flagship

BREWING NOTES

Steep 4 oz. (112 g) ground coffee in 1 qt. (0.95 L) cold water for 24 hours and
    strain off liquid and save.
Mash 60 min. @ 153°F (67°C).
Boil 90 min.
Add liquid coffee to fermentor.
Ferment until terminal, then transfer to secondary.
Condition @ 35°F (2°C) 1 week until bright.
Carbonate to 2.5 volumes (4.9 g/L) CO_2.

Glimmers of Darkness IPA *(For 5 US gallons [19 L])*

Coffee-Cacao IPA

Original gravity: 1.068 (17°P)
Final gravity: 1.019 (4.75°P)
Color: 4.92 SRM (without coffee or cacao nibs)
Bitterness: 52 IBU
ABV: 6.4%

MALTS
86% 10.5 lb. (4.8 kg) German Pilsner malt
8% 1 lb. (454 g) German Vienna malt
4% 8 oz. (225 g) Weyermann Munich malt
2% 4 oz. (112 g) crystal 30°L malt

HOPS
1.5 oz. (42 g) Pacific Gem (15% AA) @ 90 min.
1 oz. (28 g) Mosaic (12.25% AA) @ 10 min.
1.5 oz. (42 g) US Tettnang (4.5% AA) @ 2 min.
0.5 oz. (14 g) Mosaic (12.25% AA) @ whirlpool
0.5 oz. (14 g) US Tettnang (4.5% AA) @ whirlpool

ADDITIONAL INGREDIENTS
8 oz. (225 g) whole coffee beans
8 oz. (225 g) cacao nibs

YEAST
Imperial Yeast A07 Flagship

BREWING NOTES
Mash 60 min. @ 153°F (67°C).
Boil 90 min.
Ferment until terminal, then transfer to secondary.
Cold-condition on coffee beans and cacao nibs until flavor is evident.
Condition @ 35°F (2°C) until bright.
Carbonate to 2.5 volumes (4.9 g/L) CO_2.

IPA RECIPES WITH TEA

TukTukTea IPA *(For 5 US gallons [19 L])*

Thai Iced Tea IPA

Thanks to Alex Violette, Ryan Lemish, and Dave Byrn of Pasteur Street Brewing, Ho Chi Minh City, Vietnam.

Original gravity: 1.067 (16.75°P)
Final gravity: 1.019 (4.75°P)
Color: 7.81 SRM
Bitterness: 48 IBU
ABV: 6.3%

MALTS
92% 10.5 lb. (4.8 kg) Maris Otter malt
4% 8 oz. (225 g) Weyermann Munich malt
2% 4 oz. (112 g) Belgian CaraMunich malt
2% 4 oz. (112 g) Crisp 30°L crystal malt

HOPS & TEAS—VERSION 1
5.5 oz. (156 g) Fuggle (4.5% AA) @ 90 min.
1.5 oz. (42 g) oolong tea (bagged loose tea) @ 2 min.
2 oz. (56 g) East Kent Goldings (5% AA) @ 2 min.
0.5 oz. (14 g) oolong tea @ whirlpool
0.5 oz. (14 g) East Kent Goldings (5% AA) @ whirlpool

HOPS & TEAS—VERSION 2
2.4 oz. (68 g) Centennial (10% AA) @ 90 min.
1.5 oz. (42 g) Cha Dem Yen (Thai black tea), bagged @ 2 min.
2.0 oz. (56 g) Motueka (7% AA) @ 2 min.
0.5 oz. (14 g) Cha Dem Yen, bagged @ whirlpool
0.5 oz. (14 g) Motueka (7% AA) @ whirlpool

ADDITIONAL INGREDIENTS
8 oz. (225 g) lactose

YEAST
Wyeast 1056

BREWING NOTES
Mash 60 min. @ 153°F (67°C).
Add lactose to boil.
Boil 90 min.
Add bagged loose tea to whirlpool, remove before KO.
Ferment until terminal, then transfer to secondary.
Condition @ 35°F (2°C) 1 week until bright.
Carbonate to 2.5 volumes (4.9 g/L) CO_2.

TABLE 5.1 LIST OF CHOCOLATE, COFFEE, AND TEA FORMS AND THEIR ATTRIBUTES FOR USE IN BREWING IPAs

Ingredient/Form	Effect/Attribute	Combinations	Additions	Comments/Issues
Chocolate, cacao nibs	Subtle funk and flavor	Fruit, coffee, wood	Cold conditioning	Easy to measure; greatest subtlety; expensive and perishable
Chocolate, syrup or paste	Strong chocolate flavor	Fruit, coffee	Kettle, whirlpool	Often sweetened, but intense if not; difficult to dissolve—there are easier ways to introduce chocolate
Chocolate, cocoa powder	Cocoa flavor	Any cocoa flavor or combination	Kettle, whirlpool, cold conditioning	De-fatted recommended; doesn't contribute a great deal of color
Coffee, cold brew	Nuance of varietal/blend	Black IPA; lighter spice or fruit flavors	Post-fermentation, cold conditioning, packaging	Easiest and most subtle to work with; offers most possibilities
Coffee, ground	Greatest contact surface/intensity	Strong flavors, chocolate	Kettle, whirlpool, cold conditioning	Harsh if boiled or steeped overmuch; almost impossible to move around in cellar without long standpipe
Coffee, hot brew	Straight coffee flavor and effect	Black IPA	Post-fermentation, cold conditioning, packaging	Demands a dark beer; certainly the simplest way to add coffee
Coffee, whole bean	Measured effect according to contact time	Mellower flavors, chocolate, fruits, spices	Cold conditioning	Wasteful as to weight and effect, but relatively predictable and appreciable over time
Tea, black	Bold tea flavor—a statement	Black IPA	Kettle, whirlpool, cold conditioning	Most generic tea flavor; blends available to introduce subtle touch of orange, for example
Tea, fermented	Mellow, less astringent than others; more food-like	Earthy hops, sour treatments	Kettle, whirlpool, cold conditioning	Extremely unusual, I applaud you for trying
Tea, flower	Perfumy; variable as to flower	Variable as to flower	Kettle, whirlpool, cold conditioning	Tie in with allied hops
Tea, green	Grassy, straw-like	Fruit; herbal/grassy hops	Kettle, whirlpool, cold conditioning	Getting bolder . . . cultural associations

Table 5.1 continued on next page

TABLE 5.1 (cont.)

Ingredient/Form	Effect/Attribute	Combinations	Additions	Comments/Issues
Tea, herbal	Variable as to herb	Variable as to herb	Kettle, whirlpool, cold conditioning	Tie in with allied hops and terpenes
Tea, oolong	Variable	Subtle hops (or not); light fruit to allow play	Kettle, whirlpool, cold conditioning	Most variable, can be fruity, woody, or fresh according to treatment—experience and choose
Tea, smoked	Smoky, phenolic	Earthy hops, roasted malts	Kettle, whirlpool, cold conditioning	Could add a very interesting note
Tea, spice	Variable as to spice	Variable as to spice	Kettle, whirlpool, cold conditioning	Check appropriate spice contributions for reference (see table 4.2)
Tea, white	Light tea touch	Citrus, herb, sour treatment	Kettle, whirlpool, cold conditioning	Mildest touch of tea; most resilient for combination
Tea, yellow	Mild oxidation, slight color	Citrus, herb	Kettle, whirlpool, cold conditioning	Less grassy than green tea; slightly bolder than white tea; rare and expensive
Tea, yerba maté	Herbal, a bit harsh and grassy	Open-ended as to hop variety	Kettle, whirlpool, cold conditioning	A fun addition, generally quite popular

WOULD I?
WOOD-AGED
AND SOUR IPA

Among audiophiles and collectors of recordings (especially where vinyl is concerned) there's great distinction drawn between original and reissue. Original is original, of course; it's the first pressing from the authoritative and designated performance to be issued more generally for public purchase and consumption. Consider, for our purposes, the strong and hoppy pale ales produced in England in the eighteenth and nineteenth centuries and shipped to India to be the original. And then there's the reissue. It can be any number of things. It can be a cheap pressing on a budget label intended for mass market. Or it can be a beautifully reproduced copy made from the same tapes as the original, manufactured perhaps in Germany or Japan, sounding just about as good as the original, but because it's sort of an afterthought, a reconsideration of viability and promise without the stakes and limitations of the original and produced as a separate enterprise, it's a reissue. It's probably got a different label as well, or at least a paper ribbon explaining in English or Japanese or German the facts of its origin. That's what the IPAs produced in America and Australia, even India, were—a recognition of the commercial possibilities of the style after the fact. Actually, they're not even a reissue. In recording terms, they're more like Herman's Hermits singing the Beatles, an attempt to garner associative success from the original by interpretive opportunism. That's what we are, really, interpretive opportunists, taking advantage of a seemingly insatiable modern desire for the beers we produce by way of a game of stylistic telephone conducted across geographies and time, justified and explained (or maybe not) by that paper ribbon delineating what makes it different and what makes it IPA.

To my mind, the fact that they were shipped in wood is one of the compelling aspects of the original IPAs, but one that is surprisingly rarely invoked in modern interpretations. It's a matter of uncertainty how much oak character is likely to have been transmitted to the IPAs of yore from barrels lined with pitch or paraffin or otherwise. And yet it's a touch that's often enough, at least conversationally, been seized on by subsequent producers of the style (from Ballantine onward, at least), although many of them have been lost in the mists of Albion. With our modern, artisanally connected awareness of the flavors of wood in wine, spirits, and, far more recently, in beer, it might seem that this conceptual, historical link between wooden barrels and IPA would have yielded as many wood-aged IPAs as we've had the equivalent porters and stouts. But while there have been examples of wood and barrel-aged IPA, there just haven't been that many. To me it's like a lot of great ideas, obvious once suggested. Still, the future beckons.

I blame the profligacy of the bourbon industry for much of this. Not only is the single use of a barrel for making bourbon legally mandated, when most bourbon producers give up on a barrel and sell it off to somebody else for subsequent use in another industry (usually whiskey producers in Scotland and Ireland), it's typically awash in residual contents. This gives a conceptual head start to anything, in our case any beer, put into barrels so dismissed by their original users. The bold and heavy flavors of dark beers most obviously combine with the woody and alcoholic residue of bourbon left behind, but such interpretation doesn't have to end there. Not only could whiskey combine with IPA, particularly a strong IPA, but bourbon barrels, as the craft brewing industry has discovered, are not the only barrels out there.

Brewers these days are doing all sorts of crazy, and not so crazy, stuff with wood. A more complete look at this phenomenon is to be had in the book I co-wrote with Peter Bouckaert, *Wood & Beer: A Brewer's Guide* (Cantwell and Bouckaert 2016), but for the here and now I'll try to give a quick rundown on the aspects and processes most helpful to brewers of IPA who have decided to influence it with the medium of wood. This could be by the use of barrels, any number of kinds of barrels; it could be by the use of wood products such as chips, blocks, spirals, or staves; it could also be by the influence of microflora introduced to or resident in barrels into which IPA is itself introduced. It's most likely that the IPAs subjected to such treatments are going to be reasonably straight down the line, that is, hoppy and alcoholically substantial pale ales without other influence, but where brewers are concerned permutation is often the mother of invention. Why not a fruited IPA aged on fruit wood? Why not an herb or spice IPA in oak, chestnut, or amburana? Why not a wood-aged sour IPA? Why indeed. None of these are originals, either. Either that, come to think of it, or they all are.

FLAVORS FROM WOOD

It's in the Trees

We all know that trees grow concentrically, each year adding new material underneath the bark through which, for a time, nutrients flow between the roots and the leaves. Over time, of course, the trunk becomes broader owing to all this incrementally added material, the resulting growth rings testimony to the age of the tree as well as providing the grain so prized by workers of wood. Knowing no more than this one might think that any wood would be suitable for making barrels, but the fact is that oak is uniquely suited for this kind of construction and function owing to a couple of highly developed quirks in its physiology. In addition to forming rings by yearly growth, many types of trees form what are called medullary rays, emanating outward from the center of the tree and, among other things, aiding in the tree's structural integrity. In some trees, such as conifers, these rays are relatively insubstantial, sometimes as little as a single cell thick. In oaks, however, these rays provide not only the strength needed to withstand the force of wind for maybe hundreds of years, but a layer that when properly incorporated into staves cut for barrels provides a barrier imper-meable to liquid. In addition, the rings gradually adding material to the trunk grow yearly in two phases, an early-season sap-carrying layer and a more solid layer added afterward. As the year wears on that softer, more porous inner layer is filled in by outgrowths of material known as tyloses, which block the nutri-ent-conducting tubes. What has begun its function and existence as *sapwood* is then converted to *heartwood*, and that just sounds more solid, doesn't it?

The most recent layer of annual growth also happens to provide much of the flavor that we associate with oak, both in its raw, just-cut state and later, when the wood is subjected in various degree to the rigors of heat during coopering. Heat treatments include initial steaming or dry-heating so that a cut stave can be more effectively bent, and later treatments when the wood is further toasted to impart specific flavors to liquids stored within the barrel.

Before we get into what those flavors are, it's important to recognize that unlike other chapters in this book, where we've run correlation between elements of recipe formulation (specific hops and malts) or flavor-active constituents of fermentation (esters, phenols, and alcohol) and the various additional ingredients we consider adding to an IPA, when we bring wood into the equation we're talking more about a symbiosis as familiar and prized as cats supposedly were to the Egyptians. It's certainly true that many of the flavors of oak, whether raw, toasted, or charred, borrow from the descriptive language of food. But there's something atavistic about the coconut, the butterscotch, the nutmeg and cinnamon and clove of oak that speaks to us not so much as a concatenation of creative concept, but as something more fundamental and all at once. And it's been with us through much of the history of civilization.

Flavors in Oak

There are five basic groups of flavor-active compounds yielded by oak when given prolonged contact with alcoholic liquid. I'll spare you the physiological origins of each of them for now, but we will later touch a bit on how and to what degree they are brought out and developed by the heat treatments common in the manufacture of barrels.

Each of these compounds or groups of compounds can be identified by specific families of flavor. Most obvious, prevalent, and decodable in oak is vanillin. Next up are lactones, perceived as coconut, with notes, depending on type, of celery or roses. Furfurals bring a bit of baggage to evaluators of beer by their caramel and butterscotch flavors, but it's to be hoped that the truly experienced taster will know the difference between the influences of oak and those of diacetyl. The word may not come to you should you walk through an active cooperage as toasting and bending is going on, but it's the eugenols in the air that suggest clove, nutmeg, and cinnamon, the "aroma of a richly spiced cake being baked," as cooper turned historian Kenneth Kilby has observed in *The Cooper and His Trade* (Kilby 1971). And then there's guaiacol, the smoky and charred flavor imparted by bourbon barrels, for example, mainly because they've been, well, smoked and charred by direct fire.

The heat that's applied in the cooperage to aid in the bending of staves isn't always by fire. Sometimes it's by a steam or water bath, and sometimes it's by the application of radiant dry heat. Each cooperage has its own methods and standards, and its own set of descriptors when giving the potential buyer of new barrels an idea of what the different degrees of toast will smell and taste like in the finished beer, wine, or spirit aged within them. Rather than go into all that now, I'd recommend you visit the websites of any of the cooperages a simple online search will present to you, which can help you learn the differences between light, medium, and heavy toast. And, of course, there's the *Wood & Beer* book that Bouckaert and I wrote. Suffice to say that the development of all these flavors as more heat is applied is not always linear; certain flavors can increase, then diminish, then reappear in somewhat altered form as greater darkness is achieved through toasting. By contrast, some flavors simply disappear altogether and others come about as though from nowhere as a result of the prolonged application of heat.

What all this means to the brewer of IPA is that there are a lot of potential options when deciding what kind of barrel (or stave, or wooden block) to use in order to augment hoppy and alcoholic intensity and malty solidity with whatever aspects of oak or other wood have been consciously chosen. For let us not forget there are other woods used to make barrels, such as chestnut or cedar; or that there are more exotic South American woods, like amburana, used to age local spirits such as *cachaça* in a region where oak doesn't occur as often as it does further north. Now that we've brought up geography, one should mention there is variation as well among the types of oak grown and fashioned in North America, Europe, and Asia. A little research is definitely warranted.

Roll Out the Barrel

In addition to the naturally occurring compounds and flavors that can potentially come to bear on IPA (or any other beer) aged in wood, there are a few basic facts one should keep in mind about what to expect from barrels themselves. And having put it that way, the point should also be made that one of the joys of aging beer in wood is that the results are not something you can absolutely predict. Perhaps this is one of the reasons so many people these days are doing it. But let's take a look first at some of the things we know.

A barrel is an ancient technology, but like any object in the material world it has essential physical presence and characteristics. For one thing, it is necessarily of a certain size, with a corresponding mathematical relationship between its internal volume and surface area. Smaller barrels have a greater surface area in relation to volume than larger barrels, so whatever influence the wood brings to bear on the liquid temporarily housed inside, the smaller the barrel the faster the wood effect will show. The large barrels and *foeders* you see on tours of Belgian and certain American breweries have a relatively small influence on beer with regard to wood notes; they are most often employed to allow beers to mellow and meld, or to become incrementally influenced by microorganisms resident within the grain of the wood, which, over the years, has formed a particular microfloral ecosystem within that barrel. Not surprisingly, each subsequent use of a barrel lessens the effect the wood will have on the beer you put inside of it. (There's more to be said on the subject, but for most practical purposes this is the simple truth.) So, for maximum wood effect, the smaller and newer the barrel the stronger the wood flavor. For beer styles historically subject to long contact on wood amid varying conditions, these are factors to consider when incorporating such flavors.

While there are certainly those who buy new barrels in which to age their beer, it's most common among brewers to acquire barrels after they've been used in some other beverage industry (generally, this is far less expensive too). The influence of the previous contents on the flavor of anything then put inside these barrels can therefore be pretty substantial. Because bourbon barrels can only be used once to produce bourbon, they are the ones most commonly available; the first wood-aged beers of the modern age were executed in bourbon barrels. Sherry and Scotch whisky barrels are also often used; in fact, many of them will have first been used as bourbon barrels prior to sherry or Scotch. Wine barrels are used repeatedly within their own industry, but these too are eventually gotten rid of, red wine barrels far more frequently than white. In the normal course of use, any liquid will penetrate the wood of the barrel to a depth of about one to three millimeters (that's up to about ⅛"), so even if the barrel is extensively cleaned there will remain some residual wine or other spirituous material to become incorporated in any beer later introduced. The inevitable flavor addition should therefore be considered when deciding which barrels are most appropriate for aging your IPA.

Since, as briefly touched upon, barrels are made of porous material, certain precautions should be taken when aging beer or anything else within them. It's pretty common these days to see filled barrels used essentially for decoration in brewery taverns and tasting rooms—it's a rustic, sort of insta-authentic look, evoking after-hours tasting by brewers (or elves). The point is, however, that temperature and humidity are concerns that must be addressed when keeping barrels for any length of time, whether filled or not. These concerns are likely different from those that will keep customers comfortable. Not enough humidity and water will be evaporated through the wood; too much and it is alcohol that will be allowed to pass into the surroundings. While a certain amount of this liquid loss is inevitable—this is what's known poetically as the "angel's share"—it is essential to periodically top up these diminished barrels in order to keep the influence of oxygen at bay. A little oxygen creeping incrementally inward through the wood is one of the magical elements of aging beer in barrels; too much, however, and the influence of *Acetobacter* can come into excessive, vinegary play. In addition, oxygen favors the formation of esters such as ethyl lactate (buttery and creamy) and ethyl acetate (nail polish remover). Where IPA is concerned, a little bit of mellowness and roundness combined with the influence of wood is good; that tang of vinegar and the grossness of that other stuff not at all. Care must also be taken when topping not to roil the contents of a barrel in repose (or when sampling from it), but I feel that I've already gone into a bit more practical detail than this brief look at wood might warrant for the purposes of our subject.

SOUR IPA

When people within the craft brewing industry are asked what the next big thing will be once IPA has played itself out, they at least consider so-called sour beers. Never mind the ridiculousness of the notion—I always say that whatever else comes along to tickle the fancy of the peripatetic craft beer drinker, there is no "after" where IPA is concerned. What they really mean to ask is what's new, what's different, what reason should I have to look forward to the future of craft beer? For all their taxonomic amorphousness, sour beers are certainly growing as a category. And like so much else, their elements can be effectively turned to serve the brewer's purpose where the dominant style of IPA is concerned.

But first, let's see if we can even agree on what a sour beer is. Generally speaking, sour beers are any of an endless variety of beers, tracking across many different styles, that are influenced by microorganisms to register on the tongue as sour. Traditionally, a lot of these microorganisms would have occurred spontaneously in due course and, like *lambic* then and now, would have displayed a flavor complexity greater than those beers these days that are deliberately pitched with a single "sour" culture (or perhaps with a small, consciously chosen group of cultures in a particular sequence). It's important to recognize the difference in these levels of complexity when contemplating which of these flavors and effects might be appropriate for a sour beer of any type, including sour IPA. It may as well be said, many so-called sour IPAs are often not brewed as IPAs, but as less recognizable pale beers, perhaps kettle-soured and then boiled, later heavily dry-hopped for category-stretching hybrid effect.

Those who know a bit might be able to name some of these souring microorganisms. First up would likely be *Lactobacillus*. As its name indicates, this is the genus of bacteria that can usefully sour milk to make yogurt. Introduced to beer wort it can bring about a precipitous drop in pH as lactic acid is produced from fermentable sugar (and from dextrins and other starches), resulting in a beer that tastes sour. It's a strong constituent part in lambic brewing, where wort is spontaneously inoculated with naturally occurring microflora. It's what produces most kettle-soured beers, where wort is inoculated with *Lactobacillus* culture prior to being boiled. It's also the main bacteriological element of classic Berliner *weiss*. Where IPA is concerned it's important to know that *Lactobacillus* and hops don't particularly get along, because *Lactobacillus* growth is hop sensitive. Not only that, but *Lactobacillus* is also hampered by elevated levels of alcohol. You will recall that the two excesses of hops and alcohol were what discouraged spoilage while IPAs aged on those (famously disputed) protracted voyages to India.

Pediococcus would likely be the second microorganism mentioned, and what many people don't know is that this genus of lactic acid bacteria is in the same family as *Lactobacillus* (that being Lactobacillaceae). Its influence is more finicky and complex, and can in fact lead to unpleasant flavors such as diacetyl, but *Pediococcus* can also be managed; given time, such intolerable elements can be brought naturally back into line, including the disgusting ropy viscosity that can occur in aging beer due to the action of pediococci. (Time, of course, means protracted use of tank or barrel space.) As a lactic acid bacteria, *Pediococcus* can also contribute sourness to beer. There are many distinct varieties of both *Lactobacillus* and *Pediococcus*, each with somewhat different characteristics. Through most of brewing history, with some exceptions, neither of these microorganisms has been welcome in the brewery.

Particularly unwelcome among winemakers is the "wild" yeast *Brettanomyces*, but this is a fire that modern brewers have taken special joy in playing with. *Brettanomyces* (or "Brett" or "Bretta" in brewery parlance) can appear as a sweaty, goaty, wet dog kind of aroma, and also often manifests as a sort of creamy thickness. These are also elements familiar to drinkers of lambic. Like many strongly defined elements of brewing, a little *Brettanomyces* can go a long way, and the craft world of the last twenty or so years has seen its share of overdone Brett beers. Its name, in fact, derives from flavor and scientific analyses done on nineteenth-century beers produced in Britain; that's mainly porter we're talking about, but I certainly hope that gets you thinking. There's also scholarly debate these days as to whether *Brettanomyces* is capable over time of breaking down cellobiose (one of the main constituents of wood) into, among other things, alcohol. I mention this only because of the possibility, if true, that it's difficult to imagine circumstances better than a long sea voyage for favoring this kind of process. There are, however, a couple of troubling provisos where incorporating Brett into IPA is concerned. *Brettanomyces* tends to super-attenuation, and unless carefully managed will likely reduce the body of your IPA to next to nothing. In addition, over the course of a Brett fermentation enzymes within *Brettanomyces* can also reduce esters, another frequent marker for our favorite style. On the bright side, there is a particular species, *B. anomalous*, that is sometimes described as generating a pineapple effect. I'm grinning. Are you grinning?

The Antithetical and the Inevitable

There are other souring microorganisms, of course, comprised of dozens, if not hundreds, of different types, many taxonomically related to those already touched upon. One worth mentioning again here, since it constitutes a particular threat to barrel-aged beers due to its unwelcome alliance with oxygen, is *Acetobacter*, the bacteria that readily turns both sugars and alcohols into vinegar, or acetic acid. In the earlier days of consciously produced American sour beer, a certain acetic character was often tolerated, even at the judging table. This was mainly, I think, because it differentiated beers so constituted from the many that had more conventionally come before. I credit my friend Carl Kins, a Belgian banker and long-time beer judge and mentor to many of us, for kindly but insistently pointing out to us sour beer neophytes that such flavor in beer is in fact inappropriate and unpleasant, only to be tolerated in the merest presence. We know better now, or at least we fancy that we do. Even so, many American, and even Belgian, commercial examples of microbiologically complex beers are not immune to excessive acetic influence. I'd like to name a name or two, but I won't.

PUTTING A BUNG IN IT— TAKEAWAYS FROM ALL THIS PERVERSITY

In this chapter we've treated a number of things long considered enemies to sound brewing process and conceptually run them into a style traditionally devised, however imperfectly, to combat them. At the same time we've taken a look at some flavors that likely wouldn't even have shown up in early IPAs anyway. But these days we just can't stop ourselves from trying them. Perhaps we should have our heads examined (or at least talk it out over a beer), especially as there's more to be discussed, keeping the craziness of it all in perspective. I once made a Burton Union system—one could call it a Tim Burton Union system—out of pumpkins. Don't talk to me about logical extremism.

However historically dubious wood flavors in IPA may be, the richness of flavor, touch of color, and aromatic nuance provided by oak in particular is something that just works. The addition of wine and spirits from the previous use of barrels may or may not work—that's where you come in. Degree is also important. This may seem obvious, but how many times have you had a beer that made good on its flavor claims through the metaphoric use of a Tom and Jerry mallet? Conversely, one needs to be bold enough to have that flavor actually show up once one has gone to the trouble of announcing it by name or descriptor.

We've talked exclusively so far about aging IPA on or in wood, allowing for the use of barrels and foeders, as well as staves, chips, blocks, spirals, and powders. What about fermenting your IPA in wood? Brewers are generally either for this or against this depending on both fussiness and experience. It may have more conceptual appeal than anything else, but if that's your thing, or you want to claim historical precedent, have at it. When transferring your beer into a barrel for aging, whether it's fermented in wood or stainless, think about whether you want to move a certain amount of yeast along with it. This could provide just the touch of continued activity you've got in mind (ester production, say) or it could devolve to autolysis. But we are risk-takers, aren't we?

This may also seem obvious, but not all wood beers are sour beers, and vice versa. A lot of people tend to assume microbiological compromise when so certifiably unclean a surface as the inside of a barrel is combined with the otherwise sanitary medium of brewing. A lot of sour beers are brewed and aged in stainless steel tanks, and a lot of reasonably clean beers come out of barrels.

Another thing I urge you to consider when making wood-aged or sour beers is blending. Sometimes a flavor can be too strong to be allowed to lumber along (truly, no pun intended) on its own. Cut to half-strength, or even down to one-twentieth strength, with a similar or altogether other beer, what was over-bold and dominant can be tamed to nuance. For those of us able and unafraid to multitask—and really, we all do that anyway, brewing and cleaning and answering the phone and keeping up with our blogs all at the same time—blending from multiple sources is definitely the way to go. This is why it's good to keep an array of barrels that display diversity in the beers they produce. A little of this, a touch of that, and maybe a dab of something else, and you may have put together something magical. Where IPA and its microbiological challenges are concerned (see the discussion of *Lactobacillus* and *Brettanomyces* above), the answer could lie in making a straight-up IPA and blending into it a percentage of sour beer for just that tangy touch in a beer of aromatic profundity. And speaking of things none of us several years ago would have thought might work, how about an herb, fruit, spice, or tea that casts a precise line between wood, sour, and IPA (or maybe two out of three)? Delicious beer, last time I looked, was delicious beer, no matter what anyone says about where it belongs or whether it's appropriate. And that's really what we're all here to make.

IPA RECIPES USING WOOD

Single Hop Citra Belgian Session IPA *(For 5 US gallons [19 L])*

Single Hop Sour Session IPA

Thanks to Ron Jeffries of Jolly Pumpkin Artisan Ales, Dexter, Michigan, for brewing and discussing this delicious beer.

Original gravity: 1.048 (12°P)
Final gravity: 1.010 (2.5°P)
Color: 5.59 SRM
Bitterness: 54 IBU
ABV: 5%

MALTS
90% 9 lb. (4 kg) American 2-row malt
7.5% 12 oz. (340 g) crystal 30°L malt
2.5% 4 oz. (112 g) acidulated malt

HOPS
0.75 oz. (21 g) Citra (12% AA) @ 60 min.
1 oz. (28 g) Citra (12% AA) @ 30 min.
2 oz. (56 g) Citra (12% AA) @ whirlpool
6 oz. (170 g) Citra (12% AA) @ dry hop in secondary

YEAST
WLP550 Belgian Ale Yeast

BREWING NOTES

Mash 60 min. @ 153°F (67°C).

Boil 60 min.

Ferment in open fermentor, allowing temperature to rise to 78–83°F
(25–28.5°C).

Rack to biologically preconditioned (lactobacilli, pediococci, Brett) wood,
and age for 2 months, or until wild characters are evident and in balance.

Condition and dry hop with 6 oz. (170 g) Citra in secondary.

Carbonate to 2.5 volumes (4.9 g/L) CO_2.

India Pale Antitheticale *(For 5 US gallons [19 L])*

Unhopped IPA

Thanks to Will Meyers of Cambridge Brewing Co., Cambridge,
Massachusetts and Trisha Vasquez of The Herbalist, Seattle, Washington for
discussion about this recipe.

Original gravity: 1.063 (15.75°P)
Final gravity: 1.017 (4.25°P)
Color: 8.25 SRM
Bitterness: 100+, or 0, given that there aren't any hops in it, even though it
should taste really, really bitter. The rating isn't based on conventional
measure based on alpha content.
ABV: 6.8%

MALTS

89% 10 lb. (4.54 kg) Thomas Fawcett Maris Otter malt

4.5% 8 oz. (225 g) aromatic malt

4.5% 8 oz. (225 g) Weyermann Carahell malt

2% 4 oz. (112 g) Crisp 45°L crystal malt

HOPS

None

ADDITIONAL INGREDIENTS
2.0 oz. (56 g) cherry bark steeped in hot brewing liquor

0.5 oz. (14 g) dried gentian @ 10 min.

0.5 oz. (14 g) sweetgale @ 10 min.

4.0 oz. (112 g) dandelion greens @ 2 min.

0.5 oz. (14 g) yarrow @ whirlpool

0.25 oz. (7 g) angelica root @ whirlpool

½ oak barrel stave, cut into pieces small enough to fit in conditioning vessel

YEAST
Imperial Yeast A07 Flagship

BREWING NOTES
Steep cherry bark in brewing liquor >180°F (>82°C) for >1 hour.

Mash 60 min. @ 153°F (67°C).

Boil 60 min., adding herbs and greens at appropriate times.

Ferment until terminal, then transfer to secondary.

Condition on oak until flavor is evident.

Condition @ 35°F (2°C) 1 week until bright.

Carbonate to 2.5 volumes (4.9 g/L) CO_2.

WHITHER ECLECTIC IPA? THERE WILL BE HOPS!

A lot of people, many of them brewers, have a sort of love-hate thing for IPA. They love the showcasing of new hop varieties, and with all that fruitiness the opportunity to play the game of "Is There Actual Fruit in This Beer or Not?" Yet they decry the arms race of alcohol and hops. One has to admit that things have gotten a bit silly here and there. If a double IPA, for example, is not literally twice as big as a regular IPA, then a triple IPA must be some kind of double negative, that's if it is even recognizable as an IPA, or drinkable. And that is really the crux of the matter: is the beer in question delicious and balanced? Is it artful in its conception and execution? Does it advance the brewers craft and the enjoyment of the beer drinker or merely make a joke by trotting out some ingredient no one has ever heard of before, simply to say that it has now been done? We won't even get into the hazy/fruity thing here, as that is these days fast developing into its own subset of American IPA. Consider along these lines that the inquiries and explorations of this book apply to things New England or otherwise without treating the aesthetic effects of other stylistic decisions.

There was a time when to brew an IPA was to take a breath and give it a go, not knowing in advance whether people would go for a beer so markedly bitter. Then, once it became evidently clear that they would, IPA turned into one of those friends you never knew you had, but who suddenly became inseparable from you because you genuinely liked him; one who brought out a side of you that you always suspected was there, but hadn't had the courage or the opportunity to develop. And now some of us are tired of that guy, or claim we are while keeping him at least in our orbit, voicing a wistful preference for something lighter like Pilsner, or something (shudder) "sessionable." Some of us, in fairness to those who live and die by trends and numbers, have lately derived a certain amount of satisfaction—I'd even call it glee—that the IPA craze seems to be softening, or at least the steepness of its growth curve has lessened. Why, I have to ask, are so many people rooting against IPA as though it was the Dallas Cowboys, or France?

I've often said that, whatever your interpretation of who the archetypal New Yorker is, the fact remains that there are more people of every kind in New York than anywhere else in America. These are the people who make up the population of the largest city in the United States. You might not think of New York as a haven for hippies, but there are more hippies there than any other place I can think of, even if concentrations are higher in some cities of Oregon or California. The same goes for jazz buffs, or metalheads, or the people who go so far as to put on costumes for Comic-Con.

Well, IPA is still out there. It isn't going away. It is just as populous as it ever was, hidden away in plain sight in New York and San Francisco, in Portland, Maine and in Portland, Oregon. It isn't that IPA has declined, it's simply that other things have risen up with the arrival of new craft beer drinkers to put IPA into a somewhat more terrestrial perspective. There aren't fewer IPAs in our midst (or along the edges), there are just that many more stories in the Naked City of craft beer.

What I've tried to do in this book is get people thinking—brewers, beer drinkers, everyone—about what makes a great combination of flavors within the parameters established by one particular style of beer. It's a bit of a game, to be sure, squinting a bit at the science and assuming a certain artistic facility, and it's an exercise in employing free license where it rubs up against popular engagement. I can hear a few hoots, in fact, I've been hearing them through-out this process of examination, but I can also hear wheels turning, wheels that will no doubt yield some pretty interesting beer, some of which anyway is likely to be delicious. "I want beer to taste like beer," I've heard people say, mainly referring to beers that taste like s'mores or Old Bay seasoning or pho soup, but also referring to a lot of things we've at least touched upon in this book on eclectic IPA. Well, so do I—in fact, I insist on it. No matter what other ingredients might be in there, whether playing off of or contravening some basic stylistic assertion, beer should taste like beer. In Germany, with their exalted 500-year-old law, they may not be able to call the beverages treated in this book *Bier,* but given that the rest of us can, we should make certain that what we produce under our licenses or within our legally mandated 500 gallons a year actually is beer, and not a fruity, vegetable, herbal, or spicy Flavored Malt Beverage. There is presumably a different profession (or hobby) for that.

There are many other books that will help open your eyes to the possibilities of unusual ingredients for IPA, and for other beers and drinks besides. Stan Hieronymous's *Brewing Local* (2016) is a good philosophical start, while *The Homebrewer's Almanac* (Josephson et al. 2016), put together by the folks at the Scratch Brewing Company in Ava, Illinois, really gets down to it with tips for sourcing, foraging, processing, and, yes, brewing beers made with some pretty radical ingredients. Speaking of which, let's not sell our friend Randy Mosher short by failing to mention *Radical Brewing* (2004). Randy was radical before it was cool. And while only glancingly treating beer, Amy Stewart's *The Drunken Botanist* (2013) is an excellent primer on the use (and the history of use) of an awful lot of Earth's bounty.

So get out of the kitchen, er, brewery long enough to see what's available for the crafting of these and other wonderful beers. Pull over and check out that funky-looking little ethnic market in the strip mall. Those are the places with bags of dried stuff and jars imported from all over. If you are lucky enough to be in an area with lots of diversity, you can probably find the fresh stuff too. It's right over there, next to the energy drinks. Find your local quality spice market and cultivate a relationship with the people procuring the materials and executing the blends. They'll be delighted, I assure you, to talk with you about something other than potpourri. Grow your own, if you're at all inclined. It's certainly cheaper than buying the quantities you're likely to need. Those ethnic markets? They've often got seeds for sale too. A word should also be said in support of all the outfits devising, processing, sourcing, and selling natural ingredients for the use of brewers. The breadth of stuff available via the internet, shipped to your door, is astonishing and wonderful, a far cry from the lumps of cold poison with which those of us in the early days were forced to brew. And speaking of poison, if you're foraging, make certain that what you're putting in your beer is fit and appropriate for human consumption. That includes the crazy stuff you might obtain through more or less ordinary sources.

Thanks to the efforts and accomplishments of the craft industry, there will likely always be something new happening in the world of beer. And these days that likely goes double (and triple, I suppose) for IPA. From merely bold beers to fruity hops, actual fruit, and beyond, the innovation undertaken since IPA itself was rescued from the world's stylistic scrap heap is a pretty amazing story, and an enduring joy to those of us who drink them nearly every day. From those spinning tales of the Raj to those jealously guarding barstools (and opinions) in brewery taprooms and craft beer bars everywhere, IPA drinkers may differ in their stories and specific preferences, but, along with brewers eager to take chances, they are the people who have made this whole thing possible.

Where to now? That is entirely up to you . . .

APPENDIX:
FLAVOR COMPOUNDS

TERPENIC TIE-INS TO HOPS, FRUITS, HERBS, AND ALL THE REST

Any in-depth analysis of specific hop varieties and their essential oils will display landscapes of terpenic content within. By getting to know terpenes and the flavors and aromas that they suggest, you can make informed decisions not just about which hop varieties suit the tastes of your friends and customers, but which other ingredients you can choose to employ when crafting beers that will beguile and surprise them. Given the prevalence of hop character in IPA, even those that include the additional ingredients that we examine in this book, terpenic relationships between combinations of hops as well as between hops and the additional non-hop ingredients are what will likely make or break these beers.

Such in-depth analyses can show both the larger terpenic building blocks of a particular hop variety's character and the trace amounts that nudge it in various distinct directions. Nor do all hops carry the same overall oil content—pound for pound, you can extract more essential oils from some varieties compared with others. This is only one of many reasons why particular hops are suitable for particular uses, bittering, say, or as a late addition; it also presents hops through a prism with which the brewer of eclectic IPAs can make choices of both logic and artistry.

Casting an analytical eye across the profile of essential oils in hops may on the surface show particular hop varieties relatively high in one thing while low in another, perhaps indicating vast differences in effect. But if one takes a look at some of the terpenes concerned, the lack of one thing may be nearly compensated for by greater content of another, once one has evaluated the sensory terrain. In other cases, however, a doubling of those trace compounds can indicate enormous differences. As with so many things, it's all about balance and what you prefer. Spend a little time on the websites of any comprehensive hop vendor and you'll see what I mean.

The following terpenes are those most commonly measured and otherwise evaluated in beer. Each is followed by a list of fruits, herbs, and (here and there) other substances in which they occur. I rely heavily on the information available on the website of the Good Scents Company (http://thegoodscentscompany. com). Many of these lists are long. They are also repetitive, duplicating many, even dozens, of the same natural occurrences from terpene to terpene. Think of reading through them as like listening to passages of music, variations on themes that, though composed of essentially the same elements, can create vastly different effects and moods.

2-Undecanone
Alliums, banana, cayenne, clove, ginger, guava, laurel, lemongrass, marjoram, oregano, pepper (black), saffron, strawberry

beta-Pinene
Allspice, angelica, anise, basil, bay laurel, bergamot, blood orange, caraway, cardamom, carrot, cassia, celery, cinnamon, citronella, clove, coriander, cumin, currant, cypress, dill, eucalyptus, fennel, frankincense, galangal, ginger, grapefruit, guava, hyssop, juniper berry, lavender, lemon, lime, lovage, mandarin, mango, marjoram, nutmeg, orange, oregano, parsley, parsnip, pepper (black), peppermint, pines, plum, pomelo, rosemary, sage, spearmint, tamarind, tarragon, thyme, tomato, turmeric, valerian, wormwood, yarrow, yuzu

Caryophyllene
Cinnamon, galangal, juniper berry, lavender

Farnesene
Apple, basil, bay leaf, bergamot, blood orange, carrot, chamomile, cubeb, gardenia, ginger, grape, grapefruit, guava, jasmine, lavender, lemon, lime,

mandarin, nutmeg, orange, oregano, pear, pepper, spearmint, tea, thyme, witch hazel, yuzu

Geraniol
Apple, apricot, basil, bay laurel, bergamot, blackberry, blood orange, blueberry, boysenberry, cardamom, carrot, chamomile, cinnamon, citronella, clove, coriander, cumin, currant, cypress, dill, eucalyptus, fennel, frankincense, galangal, ginger, grapefruit, guava, hyssop, juniper berry, lavender, lemon, lime, lovage, mandarin, mango, marjoram, nutmeg, orange, oregano, parsley, parsnip, pepper (black), peppermint, pines, plum, pomelo, rosemary, sage, spearmint, tamarind, tarragon, thyme, tomato, turmeric, valerian, wormwood, yarrow, yuzu

Geranyl Acetate
Allspice, almond, basil, bay laurel, bergamot, blood orange, cardamom, carrot, celery, chervil, cinnamon, citronella, coffee, coriander, fig leaf, frankincense, geranium, gin, ginger, grape, grapefruit, jasmine, lavender, lemon, lemongrass, lime, lovage, mace, mandarin, marjoram, mustard, narcissus, nutmeg, orange, oregano, pepper (black), peppermint, plum, rose, rosemary, rum, sage, savory, tangerine, thyme, tomato, verbena, white wine, wormwood, yuzu

Humulene
Allspice, angelica, anise, artichoke, basil, bay laurel, bergamot, blood orange, cardamom, carrot, cassia, celery, cinnamon, citronella, clove, cubeb, currant, curry leaf, cypress, eucalyptus, fennel, firs, galangal, geranium, ginger, grapefruit, guava, hyssop, juniper berry, lavender, lemon, lemongrass, lime, mandarin, mango, marjoram, nutmeg, orange, oregano, parsley, pennyroyal, pepper (black), peppermint, pines, raspberry, rosemary, sage, spearmint, tamarind, tea, thyme, tomato, turmeric, valerian, witch hazel, wormwood, yarrow, yuzu

Limonene
Anise, caraway, cardamom, dill, fennel, pepper (black), peppermint, pines, sage, spearmint, tea tree oil

Linalool
Allspice, angelica, anise, apple, apricot, basil, bergamot, blood orange, blueberry, butter, cacao, caraway, cardamom, carrot, cassia, celery, chamomile,

cherimoya, cherry, cinnamon, citronella, clove, coriander, cranberry, cubeb, cumin, currant, curry leaf, dill, elderflower, eucalyptus, fennel, fig, frankincense, galangal, gardenia, geranium, ginger, grape, grapefruit, guava, hyssop, jasmine, lavender, lemon, lemongrass, lime, lovage, mace, mandarin, marjoram, nectarine, nutmeg, orange, oregano, papaya, parsley, patchouli, peach, pennyroyal, pepper (bell), pepper (black), peppermint, pines, pineapple, rose, rosemary, saffron, sage, spearmint, strawberry, tamarind, tarragon, tea, thyme, tomato, turmeric, valerian, wine, wormwood, yuzu

Myrcene
Allspice, angelica, anise, apricot, basil, bay laurel, bergamot, blood orange, blueberry, capsicums, caraway, cardamom, carrot, cassia, cayenne, celery, chamomile, cinnamon, citronella, coffee, coriander, cubeb, cumin, currant, curry leaf, cypress, dill, elderflower, eucalyptus, fennel, firs, galangal, geranium, ginger, grapefruit, guava, hyssop, juniper berry, lavender, lemon, lime, lovage, mace, mandarin, marjoram, nutmeg, orange, oregano, papaya, parsley, pepper (bell), pepper (black), peppermint, pines, pomelo, rosemary, saffron, sage, spearmint, tamarind, tangerine, tarragon, tea, thyme, verbena, wormwood, yarrow, yuzu

Nerol
Basil, basswood, bay laurel, bergamot, blood orange, blueberry, cardamom, carrot, cinnamon, citronella, coriander, currant, curry leaf, elderflower, eucalyptus, geranium, ginger, grape leaf, grapefruit, hyssop, jasmine, juniper berry, lavender, lemon, lime, mandarin, myrrh, nutmeg, orange, oregano, peppermint, plum, pomelo, rose, rosemary, sage, tamarind, tarragon, thyme, turmeric, witch hazel, wormwood

ESTERS, ETCETERA

Lest you get too comfortable with the subject of hop tie-ins with terpenes, we should consider a few other substances. When putting together recipes for well-hopped beer, and eclectic IPAs in particular, an understanding of the constituent aromas, flavors, and other perceptions is helpful. Contributing flavor compounds are legion in beer, of course; they are what makes variety endless and, we hope, endlessly enjoyable. Like knowing which essential oils occur in which fruit, herb, or whatever for the sake of finding a hop variety appropriate for dual use in your IPA, for a similar reason it is a good idea to consider some of the other substances that occur in the process of brewing and fermentation.

All this having been said, it's a bit of an intellectual exercise to assign quantitative weight to the words and assessments used by sensory experts to describe cognate flavors and aromas in beer. It can be important, for evaluative purposes, to be able to offer these descriptions and to identify naturally occurring substances, but what makes a good beer is the sense and sensibility of a good brewer, one who possesses the associative instincts to govern choices regarding concept, ingredients, and process. Like the lists of naturally occurring terpenes already covered, the following basic information is provided as a sort of shadow on the wall: something to think about, but not necessarily the decisive word when formulating your recipe.

Esters

Esters in beer are the aromatic result of alcohol and fatty acids coming together in chemical combination. They can be subtle and lovely, but in excess can be dominant and the sign of undisciplined process. Some beer styles are closely identified with the occurrence of particular esters. In general, ester production is dependent on wort oxygenation, fermentation temperature, starting gravity, and length of maturation. The following are among brewing's most common esters.

Ethyl Acetate

Ethyl acetate is the most common ester in beer by weight, if not necessarily by flavor effect. In elevated concentrations it suggests nail polish or solvent; with a lighter touch it can be pleasantly fruity. English sensory analysts will sometimes refer to a familiar candy, pear drops.

Isoamyl Acetate

Isoamyl acetate is the banana flavor associated with hefeweizen from southern Germany. It can sometimes seem more artificial, like candy or confectionary, suggesting marshmallow circus peanuts.

Ethyl Butyrate

Ethyl butyrate has a generally tropical effect, suggesting pineapple or Juicy Fruit® gum.

Ethyl Hexanoate (Ethyl Caproate)

Ethyl hexanoate (also called ethyl caproate) appears in lower concentrations as red apple or anise; in higher concentrations, its goaty Latin alias asserts itself.

Thiols

Thiols, also known as mercaptans, are organosulfur compounds where sulfur stands in for oxygen in the hydroxyl group of alcohol. Many thiols carry unpleasant connotations: skunk musk, strong garlic, and the substance added to odorless natural gas to aid in identifying leaks. The fracking fields of today can be sadly redolent of mercaptan. Other, gentler ones embody pleasant fruit flavors that when occurring in fermentation can add a nice touch to the types of beer we consider in this book. A few thiols of the latter type follow.

3-Mercaptohexanol

3-Mercaptohexanol (or 3-mercapto-1-hexanol) occurs naturally in grapefruit juice, passion fruit, and red wine.

3-Mercaptohexyl Acetate

3-Mercaptohexyl acetate occurs in passion fruit and wine.

4-Mercapto-4-methylpentan-2-one

4-Mercapto-4-methylpentan-2-one (4MMP) occurs in grapefruit juice, white wine, and yuzu peel oil.

Thioesters

Thioesters are the result of esterification between carboxylic acid and a thiol (once more with sulfur taking the place of oxygen), and of fatty acid metabolism. Their contribution to beer flavor can be all over the map depending on concentration, and hence can suggest boiled beef, strawberry, melon, or coffee all in a single package.

Lactones

Lactones are often considered in the use of wood in aging beers, and show up as the coconut constituent of oak flavor. They also occur in the musk-like oil of angelica root as well as in celery, lovage, and sweet woodruff.

Aldehydes

Like esters, aldehydes are common aroma compounds used in the formulation of perfumes. Aldehydes occur naturally in anise, cedar, cilantro, cinnamon, citrus, and many flowers such as rose, jasmine, iris, honeysuckle, and lily of the valley. While some common aldehydes, such as formaldehyde and acetaldehyde, would be considered unpleasant accents in beer, some can suggest the warmth and richness of oak due to vanillin and the buttery/caramel elements inherent in furfural.

BIBLIOGRAPHY

Andre, Christelle M., Jean-Francois Hausman, and Gea Guerriero. 2016. *"Cannabis Sativa*: The Plant of the Thousand and One Molecules." *Frontiers in Plant Science* 7:19. doi:10.3389/fpls.2016.00019.

Bamforth, Charles W. 2012. "Aldehydes." In *Oxford Companion to Beer*, edited by Garret Oliver. New York: Oxford University Press.

Bruman, Henry J. 2000. *Alcohol in Ancient Mexico*. Salt Lake City: University of Utah Press.

Buhner, Stephen H. 1998. *Sacred and Herbal Healing Beers: The Secrets of Ancient Fermentation*. Boulder: Siris Books.

Bushman, Zachary. 2015. "Ester Production in Fermentation." *Gastronexus* (blog). Gastrograph AI, September 21. http://www.gastrograph.com/blogs/gastronexus/ester-production-in-fermentation.html.

Cantwell, Dick, and Peter Bouckaert. 2016. *Wood & Beer: A Brewer's Guide*. Boulder: Brewers Publications.

Carpenter, Dave. 2015. "Off-Flavor: Phenolic." *Craft Beer & Brewing Magazine*, July 21. http://beerandbrewing.com/off-flavor-phenolic/.

Eckhardt, Fred. 1989. *The Essentials of Beer Style: A Catalog of Classic Beer Styles for Brewers and Beer Enthusiasts*. Fred Eckhardt Communications.

Evans, Evan. 2012. "Maillard Reaction." In *Oxford Companion to Beer*, edited by Garret Oliver. New York: Oxford University Press.

Gascoyne, Kevin, François Marchand, Jasmin Desharnais, and Hugo Américi. 2014. *Tea: History, Terroirs, Varieties*. 2nd ed. Richmond Hill, ON: Firefly Books.

Glaser, Greg. 2000. "The Late, Great Ballantine." *Modern Brewery Age*, March 27.

Hieronymus, Stan. 2016. *Brewing Local: American-Grown Beer*. Boulder: Brewers Publications.

———. 2016. "Hops Oils and Aromas: Uncharted Waters." *Craft Beer & Brewing Magazine*. March 16. https://beerandbrewing.com/hops-oils--aroma-uncharted-waters/.

Hough, J.S., D.E. Briggs, R. Stevens, and T.W. Young. 1982. *Hopped Wort and Beer*. Vol. 2 of *Malting and Brewing Science*. London: Chapman and Hall.

Hull, Grady. 2008. "Olive Oil Addition to Yeast as an Alternative to Wort Aeration." *Technical Quarterly of the Master Brewers Association of the Americas* 45(1):17–23.

Jackson, Michael. 1982. *The World Guide to Beer*. London: New Burlington Books.

Josephson, Marika, Aaron Kleidon, and Ryan Tockstein. 2016. *The Homebrewer's Almanac: A Seasonal Guide to Making Your Own Beer from Scratch*. New York: The Countryman Press.

Karp, David. 2004. "A Finicky Fruit Is Sweet When Coddled." *New York Times*, September 1. http://www.nytimes.com/2004/09/01/dining/a-finicky-fruit-is-sweet-when-coddled.html.

Khatchadourian, Raffi. 2009. "The Taste Makers." *New Yorker*, November 23. http://www.newyorker.com/magazine/2009/11/23/the-taste-makers.

Kilby, Kenneth. 1971 (Reprint 1989). *The Cooper and His Trade*. Fresno, CA: Linden Publishing Co.

Lund, Marianne, Signe Hoff, René Lametsch, and Mogens Andersen. 2012. "Thiols During Production and Storage of Beer." Abstract 69. Technical Session 20: Finishing and Stability Session. Paper presented at the World Brewing Congress, Portland, August 1.

McDonough, Elise. 2016. "Which Fat Absorbs THC Best?" *High Times*, June 1. http://hightimes.com/edibles/which-fat-absorbs-thc-best/.

Miller, Dave. 1988. *The Complete Handbook of Home Brewing*. North Adams, MA: Storey Communications.

Mosher, Randy. 2004. *Radical Brewing: Tales and World-Altering Meditations in a Glass*. Boulder: Brewers Publications.

Noonan, Gregory J. 1996. *New Brewing Lager Beer: The Most Comprehensive Book for Home and Microbrewers*. Rev. ed. Boulder: Brewers Publications.

Papazian, Charlie. 1984. *The Complete Joy of Home Brewing*. New York: Avon Books.

Pittman, Steven J. 2012. "Terpenes." In *Oxford Companion to Beer*, edited by Garret Oliver. New York: Oxford University Press.

Rose, Brent. 2014. "How Pabst Brought a 136-Year-Old Beer Back from the Dead." Gizmodo, August 29. http://gizmodo.com/how-pabst-brought-a-136-year-old-beer-back-from-the-dea-1628690352.

Seabrook, John. 2002. "The Fruit Detective." *New Yorker*, August 19. http://www.newyorker.com/magazine/2002/08/19/the-fruit-detective.

Shellhammer, Thomas H. 2014. "Hop Quality—A Brewer's Perspective." Presentation. University of Vermont 5th Annual Hops Conference, Burlington, VT, February 27.

Sorini, Marc and Vanessa K. Burrows. 2017. "Craft Beer and Marijuana." *New Brewer*, November/December.

Steele, Mitch. 2012. *IPA: Brewing Techniques, Recipes and the Evolution of India Pale Ale.* Boulder: Brewers Publications.

Stewart, Amy. 2013. *The Drunken Botanist: The Plants that Create the World's Great Drinks.* Chapel Hill, NC: Algonquin Books.

Sumpson, Jon. 2014. "Weed-infused Beer Is a Real Thing, and We Tell You How to Make It." Food and Drink. Thrillist, February 23. http://www.thrillist.com/drink/nation/how-to-make-pot-infused-beer-thrillist-nation/.

White, Chris, and Jamil Zainasheff. 2010. *Yeast: The Practical Guide to Beer Fermentation.* Boulder: Brewers Publications.

INDEX

ABOUT THE AUTHOR

Industry veteran Dick Cantwell heads up brewing operations at Magnolia Brewing Co. in San Francisco. Previously he was brewmaster at Elysian Brewing in Seattle, during which time Elysian was awarded Large Brewpub of the Year at the Great American Beer Festival® on three occasions (1999, 2003, and 2004). Also in 2004, Cantwell received the Brewers Associations' Russell Schehrer Award for Innovation in Brewing. He has co-authored *Barley Wine* with Fal Allen and *Wood & Beer* with New Belgium's Peter Bouckaert, and is editor of the second edition *Brewers Association's Guide to Starting Your Own Brewery*. He divides his time between Seattle and San Francisco.